When Your Soul
Enters the Iron

Finding God to Be Enough
When the Pain Doesn't Go Away

Mark Fischer with Rob Fischer

Table of Contents

Acknowledgements: I could not have written this book without the help of some dear friends.

Our friends, Roy and Karin Clinesmith have stood with us for many years. Karin's expertise in editing my rough draft is a gift from God. Karin, I am deeply grateful for all your hard work. I also wish to thank Carol Jingling for her diligent and gracious work in typing the manuscript. I offer many thanks to Erin Schwab for her careful expertise in proofing this work.

I'm deeply thankful to my brother, Rob, who has gone the extra mile in the final editing of this book. Because we grew up together, Rob knows me like few others. Thanks Rob for your love, understanding, and hard work. And I wish to thank Rob's daughter Heather Wilbur for her creative expertise in the cover design.

My dear friend Gwen Allmon wrote the forward. Thank you, Gwen, for your gracious words and for your encouraging letters through the years.

I especially give thanks to my dear wife, Denese, who helped type and critique the manuscript. Mostly, I thank her for her love, patience, service and faithfulness as my wife. She has stood with me through it all. I love you, Denese! I also want to thank my children and extended family for their love and support through the years.

And finally with deepest gratitude beyond words, I thank the God and Father of our Lord Jesus Christ. To You I give all the glory!

Prologue: It was my privilege to have Mark Fischer as my pastor. Mark was affiliated with Village Missions and shepherded our rural congregation in Montana for several years. And rich years they were for our little flock! I still keep valued notes, which I took, outlining deep lessons from Mark's preaching. When the pastorate became too onerous for his strength and he had to leave, Mark and his devoted wife, Denese, remained our cherished friends.

Mark is a servant who truly serves his Lord. In spite of disability, he yearned to be about his Father's business. While continuing to seek healing from the Great Physician, he nonetheless said, "Yes, my Lord," to his affliction. Since he could no longer cope with the stresses of a pastorate, in the quiet of his restricted orbit at home, he ministered to individuals whom his Lord brought to him. Mark started a written record of the profound lessons that God was teaching him through his adversity. In time, these took shape into the book you are now holding.

Back in the Middle Ages, forerunners of today's scientists had the conviction that if they could only find the right combination of base metals and heat them to the right degree, they could transmute them into gold. For these alchemists, it was, of course, a vain pursuit. But in the spiritual realm, it is as if Mark has taken the iron that entered his soul and coupled it with the base materials of pain, weakness and incapacity. Then, in the fires of his adversity and by God's grace, he has transmuted these into gold—for this book is pure gold. These profound, relevant insights were developed out of his suffering. His words speak powerfully because they were forged in the fires of suffering. I am reminded of Isaiah 45:3, "I will give you the treasures of darkness; riches stored in secret places, so that you may know that I am the Lord."

In the providence of God, Mark's manuscript came to me during a season of darkness in my own life, making it doubly meaningful. I recommend this book to you from a full and grateful heart.—*Gwen Allmon*

Introduction: My chief purpose in writing this book is to come along side you through the fellowship of suffering. You may be looking for answers, and I hope many of your questions will be answered in this book. But beyond the mere words on these pages, please allow me to walk together with you to the One who alone has all the answers. God has answers beyond those of the intellect and even of the heart. May you know and rest in the Most High God, who loves you, cares for you, and even likes you!

Knowing God is ultimately more profound and more satisfying than having all our difficult questions answered. This is precisely what God did with Job when he was in the middle of his deep, agonizing suffering. After 37 chapters of questions and pleas for answers, God completely satisfied all of Job's searching questions when He put His hands on Job's cheeks and said, "Look into my eyes and see your God."

Chapter 1.
When Your Soul Enters the Iron

It wasn't the path you had chosen. Your desires and dreams carried your thoughts and plans down another trail, one with vistas of hope and fulfillment. You believed in God, you embraced His promises, you sought His will. You believed the concept that "God loves you and has a wonderful plan for your life." Sure you made a few bad choices along the way—everybody does. But you just never saw this coming.

Job said it best, "I was at ease, but he shattered me, and He has grasped me by the neck and shaken me to pieces; He has set me up as His target." (Job 16:12 NKJV) Looking back, it was as if God had a bulls-eye on your back. His arrow hit the mark. He reeled you in, grabbed you by the neck and shook you. Your life is shattered.

I'm not talking about acute pain, pain that can be very intense, but subsides in a relatively short period of time. The pain I'm referring to is not like stepping on a nail or experiencing a kidney stone, (unless you keep getting them). I'm talking about *chronic pain*, whether it is physical, mental or emotional. Chronic pain stays with you for a long time. It grabs you by the neck and won't let you go. Chronic pain is relentless and life altering. Chronic pain redefines your life, because it takes you on a different path, one you didn't choose.

Oh yes, maybe you were indirectly involved with the turn of events, like driving too fast, or not taking care of your health or marriage, but you would never have *chosen* these events for yourself. Perhaps you weren't even indirectly involved. We have no control over events like the sudden death of a child, an accident caused by a drunk driver, a stubborn and mysterious illness: Multiple Sclerosis (MS), Lyme's disease, Fibromyalgia (FMS), or a chemical imbalance that sends you into depression. Perhaps you are living in a part of the world where persecution for your faith hounds you daily. Or maybe your chronic pain was brought on directly by you. But, whatever the cause, you now find yourself in a long term relationship with pain and suffering you never wanted.

His Soul Entered the Iron. The title of this book comes from the Old Testament account of Joseph's imprisonment. In Psalm 105:18 (NIV) we read, "They bruised his feet with shackles, his neck was put in irons." The literal rendering of the second part of that verse, "his neck was put in irons," is, "his soul entered the iron." The Hebrew word for *neck* and *soul* both come from the same word *nephesh*.

The neck is a physical replica of the soul. Through the neck air, food and water pass. The neck is the channel of the breath of life. When God created Adam, He breathed into him and he became a living soul.

The soul is the essence and animation of who you are as a person. The Bible says a soul can be hungry, thirsty, and satisfied. The soul can sin, be unsettled, or made bitter. When Jesus saves a soul, He saves the whole person—body, mind, emotions and will.

Charles Spurgeon rightly said, "The whole person is denoted by the soul, because the soul of the captive suffers still more than the body. Imprisonment is one of the most severe trials to the soul...."[1] "His soul entered the iron." Until we have experienced the "iron" invading our soul, we cannot conceive of that sickness of heart, which at times will steal upon the patient sufferer. We cannot imagine that sense of loneliness; that sense of deep loss, which comes from hopes deferred and wishes shattered. And we cannot fathom the heartlessness of the world, or worse yet, the cruel abandonment of friends and family.

Joseph is a clear Biblical example to us of a *chronic sufferer*.[2] As one of the 12 sons of Jacob (Israel), he was despised by his older brothers probably for at least three reasons: 1) parental favoritism; 2) tattling; 3) and Joseph's dreams in which he reigned over his brothers.[3]

Remember Joseph was only 17 years old when all this went down.[4] His brothers were jealous of him and hated him so much that their initial plan was to kill him.[5] Killing him may have been easier on Joseph in light of what he would end up going through. Their plan B was throwing him stripped and without water into a pit. Finally, Joseph's brothers carried out plan C selling him to Ishmaelite slave traders who sold him to the Egyptian, Potiphar. Without going into all the details here, note that Joseph went into prison at age 17 and came out at age 30,[6] though technically, he never really was totally released from Egypt (the land of his captivity) until he died.

Now, we know the end of this story and how it turned out good for Joseph. Yet we often overlook all that Joseph experienced in his suffering. Think of how he must have agonized over being rejected by his own brothers and being separated from his father! Joseph was truly alone. He was restricted, hampered and confined; he was no doubt afraid; he was tempted severely; misunderstood; and forgotten.

Joseph was chained in a foreign prison with his feet fettered or shackled. His feet were *afflicted* by the chains—they were hurt—probably causing many sleepless nights—cold, bloody, and raw. Perhaps the chains may have permanently damaged his ankles, we don't know. They clamped his neck in an iron collar. They clamped iron around his throat! Any movement was restricted. Eating and drinking were hampered. Days turned into long nights, which turned into weeks, which turned into months, which turned into years, with no end in sight.

Apparently, after a time, he was given work to do, but most likely returned to chains at night. Moses spoke of this and the following enslavement of the nation of Israel as a whole. "But as for you, the Lord took you and brought you out of the iron-smelting furnace, out of Egypt, to be the people of His inheritance, as you now are." (Deuteronomy 4:20 NIV) God puts His people through an *iron-smelting furnace of affliction* to purify and ultimately bless us. Do we understand this?

My point is this—*Joseph's soul entered the iron.* His confinement and the pain of his chronic suffering, in one sense, began to define him—*Joseph the prisoner.* He must have longed for his God-given dreams to come true, but he entered a path of suffering he never wanted or asked for.

If you were to ask a chronic sufferer, "What's your main pain or problem?" you will probably hear, "The anguish of my soul." Though the initial pain may be in a part of the body, or a recurring thought of our mind, or a festering raw emotion, the pain radiates out to impact relationships, job, finances, health and many other things. Chronic pain affects the total person. In chronic pain there's an anguish of soul. The Psalmist said of Joseph, "Until the time that His Word came to pass, the Word of the Lord tested him." (Psalm 105:19 NASB)

In the end we must see two things: 1) God's timing "until"; and 2) God's Word "tests" us. Without denying the reality of the pain, we see a greater reality—God's Word, His promises and His commands. In other words we can say, "Here's what is happening to me, but here's what God says to me." And behind God's Word is God himself. "The Lord was with Joseph…" (Genesis 39:2 NIV) Wow! That changes everything. Any trial, *plus God*, is far better than no trial without God. *Do you believe that?*

The story of Joseph turned out very, very well because God was with him. For all of us there is an "until", an ultimate end to the trials, but do we believe and know by experience that God is present with us now? "Bless the Lord, O my soul, and forget not all His benefits, who forgives all your iniquity, who heals all your diseases, who redeems your life from the pit, who crowns you with steadfast love and mercy, who satisfies you with good so that your youth is renewed like the eagle's." (Psalm 103:1-5 ESV)

If you are reading this and you know and believe that Jesus is your Savior, please recognize that there must come a point in our trials of faith that we look deeply into the face of God and see His sovereign delight in us. Not that the trials aren't hard, but God is working through them a much greater good. After incredible trials over many years Joseph confidently said to his brothers: "Do not be afraid, for am I in God's place? But, as for you, you meant evil against me, but God meant it for good, in order to bring about as it is this day, to save many people alive." (Genesis 50:19-20 NKJV)

Yes, the man whose soul entered the iron of chronic pain and trial did not deny its reality, but he embraced the greater reality that God is in His rightful place as Sovereign Lord. He trusted God and waited with anticipation.

Dear Friend, has your soul entered the iron of pain? Can you identify with Joseph? It's as if he is saying—I don't simply *feel* pain, I *am* pain. Please remember, Jesus entered the iron, too. Nailed to a cross with iron nails, He has suffered with you and He has not left you alone!

Would you work with me through these pages as together we see the wisdom of God in these issues of chronic pain? We're not looking for pat answers that may be true, but leave us empty. What we need is an investment of love and compassion. And sometimes it's without a word that we are most comforted. The Lord knows your pain and enters into it with you.

Chapter 2.
An Unwanted Calling

A few years ago two men crossed my path. Both were kind, godly men. They loved God and attended the same church. Both had loving, faithful wives. But there was a great difference between the two. One had had an accident, a freak accident as a young man—he was never the same again. He suffered his whole life from this experience. Now, as an older man, I came to know him. The last year of his life was spent in the hospital. I visited him often. His was a painful struggle. After he died, his wife told me that his last year had genuinely been the best year of their marriage.

The second man was about 10 years older than the first. We were talking one day about the first man's life of struggle and premature death. This second gentleman said, "Mark, I have never suffered or been in pain any day of my life." He was not bragging. He was thankful and yet puzzled. Why the vast difference between these two men's experience? About a year later he went out to mow the lawn and at 77 years of age fell over dead from a heart attack. He never did suffer. I've often thought about this disparity between the two men's experiences.

It seems that God calls some people to a life of pain and suffering. I think of the Apostle Paul at his conversion. First, he suffered from temporary blindness. He was told to go "see" Ananias who is instructed by God to lay hands on him. We read what God told Ananias to tell Paul, "But the Lord said to him,

'Go', for he [Paul] is a chosen instrument of Mine, to bear My Name before the Gentiles and Kings and the Sons of Israel; for I will show him how much he must suffer for my Name's sake." (Acts 9:15-16 NASB)

> Afflictions through pain and suffering were Paul's God-given destiny.[7] Paul said:
>
> (I have) been put in jail more often, been whipped times without number, and faced death again and again. Five different times the Jews gave me thirty-nine lashes. Three times I was beaten with rods. Once I was stoned. Three times I was ship-wrecked. Once I spent a whole night and day adrift at sea. I have traveled many weary miles. I have faced danger from flooded rivers and from robbers. I have faced danger from my own people, the Jews, as well as from the Gentiles. I have faced danger in the cities, in the deserts, and on stormy seas. And I have faced danger from men who claim to be Christians, but are not. I have lived in weariness and pain and sleepless nights. Often I have been hungry and thirsty and have gone without food. Often I have shivered with cold, without enough clothing to keep me warm. Then besides all this, I have the daily burden of how the churches are getting along. (2 Corinthians 11:23-28 NLT)

Most likely Paul's last trial was his most difficult. The point—Paul had a calling on his life, from God, to suffer.

It seems that everyone suffers to some degree, just by virtue of living on planet earth. As part of the human race, sin has infected and affected everyone and everything. Even the second man I mentioned earlier probably did suffer to some degree, but his suffering was overshadowed by his good health and positive outlook. Even so, in his mind, he really wasn't called to a life of pain.

It is important to understand the nature of God's callings on our lives. There is a universal call to all mankind to come to God in repentance and faith in Jesus Christ. There is a narrower call of election—"Many are called but few are chosen." Paul tells us in Romans that those who are chosen are *justified and glorified*. God's choice of us is an irrevocable calling, resulting in genuine faith. Within that divine calling are many other callings: the call to be single or married; the call to the pastorate; the call to "secular" work; the call to go to the mission field and the call to stay and support those who go.

These other callings may change during our lifetime. A single person, after being called to be single for a season may get married. A married person may lose a spouse and be called to singleness. A missionary may be called home, etc. And then some are called to health and some are called to pain and suffering. Or, vice versa—one who has suffered for many years may actually be healed and enjoy good health.

As hard as it is for us to comprehend—God calls some people to chronic pain and suffering. We've already cited the Apostle Paul. Someone might argue that his pain was different because it was pain from persecution, and yet Scripture tells us that he considered all things to be "loss in view of the surpassing value of knowing Christ Jesus my Lord." (Philippians 3:7)

We also read earlier that Paul lived in "weariness and pain and sleepless nights." That sounds a lot like FMS, Chronic Fatigue, Hepatitis, Lyme's disease, Lupus, MS or a myriad of other illnesses. To the one suffering, whether it came from persecution, someone's foolishness, a virus, bacteria or injury, pain is pain—it still hurts and may even display the exact same symptoms regardless of the cause.

Here's the point! God is the Most High God, sovereign and wise in all His works among humanity and especially in the life of the believer.

We think that the worst we can experience in life is pain and suffering. In contrast, *my* desires for *my* life include: comfort, pleasure, happiness and prosperity. As I read Scripture, however, God's list looks a little different. His list of good things for my life consists of: His glory, holiness, grace, faith, love, comfort, pleasure, joy, and blessings. What if from God's perspective His glory is more important than my pain-free life? Does that mean He loves me any less? We'll take that up in the coming chapter.

But for now, let's take faith and pleasure as examples that are high on God's list for our lives. We understand that, within His glory, an intimate relationship is what He desires with us above all else. He proved that by providing reconciliation for us through the death of His Son on the Cross. And that relationship is what we must understand when we use the term "faith". So, when we say, "My faith is growing," what we're really saying is, "My relationship with God is growing."

If God desires, sometimes He will sacrifice lesser things to accomplish the greater good. He will sometimes sacrifice health, long life, other relationships, prosperity and comfort or even sanity for the greater good of our intimate relationship with Him, which also transcends this life. So we can understand why Peter said, "Beloved, do not be surprised at the fiery ordeal among you, which comes upon you for your testing, as though some strange thing were happening to you." (1 Peter 4:12 NASB)

When trials of chronic pain come our way, we should not think it a strange thing, because God said they would come. We don't need to seek suffering in some sadistic or masochistic way—suffering *will* come. Trials of faith come in order to bring us closer to God. I find it insightful that most Christians I've talked with say of a trial, "I never want to go through that again! The pain was excruciating and yet afterward I saw how my suffering brought me closer to God, for which I'm eternally grateful."

The other example from God's list of good things for my life is pleasure. This is one we often only look at negatively (or with guilt). But, let's stand back and look at the bigger picture. Some might be surprised to see pleasure at the top of God's favorite list! But I believe that God created us for mutual pleasure—both His and ours. Pleasure is very important to God. In fact He loves it. The Psalmist says, "For the Lord takes pleasure in His people; He will beautify the afflicted ones with salvation." (Psalm 149:4 NASB) God created us for His pleasure—it's our calling in life to bring Him pleasure.

God delights in us—He even likes us! Now sin interrupted that. Prideful human rebellion displeased God—it brought His displeasure and His justice. God's justice also brings Him pleasure—not because of what it does *to* people, but because of what it does for His holiness and *for* people. His holiness is His spiritual vitality and separateness from sin. We can be very grateful for this because it provides hope and a way out of the spiritual consequences of sin. When we are rightly related to God and growing in that faith relationship, He is delighted and so are we.

God also built us to enjoy pleasure. He's not a kill-joy. Solomon says, "Here is what I have seen to be good and fitting; to eat, to drink and enjoy oneself in all one's labor, in which he toils under the sun, during the few years of his life which God has given him; for this is his reward." (Ecclesiastes 5:18 NASB) God calls us to work and He wants us to enjoy the fruit of our labor.

And yet, even more important and pleasurable is this, "You will make known to me the path of life; in your presence is fullness of joy; in your right hand there are pleasures forevermore." (Psalm 16:11NASB) There is no joy and pleasure that can truly satisfy us except the company of God and to be in right relationship with Him.

So, if God sacrifices temporary things for eternal things is He not wise in doing so? If He removes lesser pleasures to give us greater and longer lasting pleasures, is He not wise? Again, that is why Paul said, "I've suffered the loss of all things gladly so I can gain Christ." If we are called to a relationship with God, we must understand what that means. Peter wrote, "After you have suffered for a little while, the God of all grace, who called you to His eternal glory in Christ, will *Himself* [personally] perfect, confirm, strengthen, and establish you." (1 Peter 5:10 NASB)

In fact, sometimes we are given the choice to choose a greater pleasure over a lesser one. Moses exemplifies this:

By faith, Moses, when he had grown up, refused to be called the son of Pharaoh's daughter, *choosing* rather, to endure ill-treatment with the people of God, than to enjoy the passing pleasures of sin, considering the reproach of Christ greater riches than the treasures of

Egypt; for he was looking to the reward. (Hebrews 11:24-26 NASB)

Moses made a choice for *ill-treatment* instead of the temporary pleasures of sin. He chose to suffer in the moment for greater rewards—both his reward to come in heaven and the fellowship of suffering *with* Christ and the people of God now. To suffer reproach was to be identified in relationship with Christ and His family. That was more pleasurable than being a royal Egyptian son, enjoying sin's pleasures, or owning the treasures of Egypt. Sin has an instant gratification of pleasure, but choosing God brings an infinite and eternal pleasure of the enjoyment of His presence. There are many spiritual tools for overcoming sin. Maybe we should use this tool of finding pleasure in God more often.

Are you called by God to suffer chronic pain at this time? Remember, if suffering has no purpose, it is unbearable. But if in your suffering you can see a purposeful God, then your suffering is bearable because God renders it meaningful. At the moment, you may have no other purpose for your trial than that God has allowed it. I think it was Fredrick Buechner who said, "God doesn't reveal his grand design—He reveals Himself." John of Avila said, "I pray God may open your eyes and let you see what hidden treasures He bestows on us in the trials from which the world thinks only to flee."[8]

Jesus Christ is our *hidden treasure*. If there were no other reason for my suffering, than that God called me to it, wouldn't that be sufficient? Think about it, Jesus did not change the world through His *miracles*, but by *His suffering*. Oh that I may "know Him and the fellowship of His suffering."

We find it difficult sometimes in the midst of a trial to embrace God's call of suffering, but it is not impossible. It is a great privilege to be called by God to suffer. This is an honor. I pray that we can recognize this truth as we move ahead. Don't give up. Pursue God in your pain; that is wisdom.

Chapter 3.
The Difficult Question of 'Why'?

"To our heart-wrenched cries of 'why?' God's ultimate answer is 'Jesus'. The times when you and I can't trace His hand of purpose, we must trust His heart of love!"[9]

I wonder how often Joseph cried out to God, "Why?" during his long nights in prison? "Why did God allow this?" "Why me?" "Why so long?" "Why doesn't He answer my prayer?" "Why won't He set me free?" Sometimes God does answer some of these questions through the good that comes from pain. Sometimes God doesn't tell us "why", at least not on this side of heaven. Sometimes the plan of God is so vast, detailed and intertwined we wouldn't be able to understand even if He did tell us.

The question "Why?" is very personal. As we mentioned in the last chapter, suffering requires meaning and purpose. As rational creatures, we often demand an answer from God. After all, He is all-wise, all-knowing, all-powerful, all-loving, and all-good. So, we may ask, "Why did I get an illness of pain that no one understands or can diagnose?" "Why was my child born with a severe abnormality?" "Why did my mother suffer from debilitating depression?" We want to understand why we and those we love must endure such suffering. We want reasons and meaning and we want the meaning to out-weigh the pain.

The question "Why?" is a prayer of soul-anguish. That prayer comes from the core of our lives, because it questions the God we say we believe in. If He is good, why did bad happen? If He is all-powerful, why didn't He stop it in the first place? Can we really trust a God whom we can't understand? The resounding answer is yes! You see, God is not *irrational*. He just works beyond the realm of our rationale.

One of the most profound things God does is to bring us face to face with Himself rather than explain everything He does. Please don't get me wrong. He explains more than we study to know or care to believe. The Scriptures are full of explanations and principles of God's actions. In fact, in the prophetic Word, He tells us much of what He is going to do, often in great detail before it happens. Jesus told his disciples a number of times why they were headed to Jerusalem. He said He would suffer many things, be killed and rise the third day. Maybe they didn't want to hear or believe about His suffering and death because they wanted Him to overthrow Rome and set up His Kingdom. His dying just wasn't in *their* plans. But everything about Jesus' death was exactly according to God's plans. The Scripture *had* to be fulfilled.

Other explanations and principles that may help us understand our "Why?" questions include: 1) God's ways and thoughts are higher than ours. He is personal, but also transcendent—way above us; 2) faith grows in trials. We learn to trust Him; 3) the character of Christ is developed during trials of faith. We develop perseverance, patience, hope and love; 4) the comfort we receive from God helps us comfort others; 5) adversity is a framework from which we can edify the body of Christ, for when one member suffers, all suffer; 6) trials purify us from sin in particular, but also from *good* things that rob us of the *best* things. And there are many other legitimate reasons why God brings about, or allows suffering in our lives.

This might be a good time to ask who actually afflicted us, God or Satan. The first answer is that we may not always know. Job didn't know that Satan was actually the culprit behind his afflictions. We don't always know the exact lines of activity in the angelic and divine realm.

Paul wrote that the "thorn in the flesh" that tormented him was a messenger of Satan. He knew it was Satan afflicting him. Yet, the wording in 2 Corinthians 12 implies that God superintended Paul's affliction to keep him from being prideful of the great revelations he was allowed to see. Satan would have encouraged pride, not kept him from it.

Then Paul prayed to God for the removal of his affliction three times and the Sovereign God, who can answer any prayer instantly and completely, basically said, "No, instead, I'll give you something better than healing—a measure of weakness (or humility) surrounded and infused with my power of grace." Better to be humble and weak, but cloaked in God's loving favor, which is divinely powerful, than to be proud and humanly strong, but with no divine favor. The saying is true, "The quickest way to the heart is through a wound."

So, if God tells us who initiated or brought about our affliction, that's good. If he doesn't tell us, that's okay too, because as God's child nothing happens to us that does not come through God's good intentions and permission. "And we know that God causes all things to work together for good to those who love God, to those who are called according to *His purpose*." (Romans 8:28)

"What then shall we say to these things? If God is for us, who is against us?" (Romans 8:31) That's a powerful statement on our behalf spoken by God Himself. God is for us! We must deposit that in our *faith bank* for future times of withdrawal. God is for us! He's not against us. In the dark nights of the soul when our faith is attacked from all sides and the reality of chronic pain rages on—the even greater reality, the unseen reality is—God is for us! *He's for us!!* He's on our side working on our behalf in ways of grace and love and goodness.

"Surely goodness and mercy shall follow me all the days of my life and I will dwell in His presence forever." (Psalm 23:6) Like the apostle Paul, we must be convinced of this, that nothing can separate us from His infinite and intimate love for us, not even our chronic hurt that is unrelenting and maybe even intensifying. Can we believe God when He speaks truth over our pain without removing it? God says to me, "Mark, I love you, I am for you!"

Isaiah, speaking of God's great goodness to the nation of Israel, said, "In all their affliction He was afflicted, and the angel of His presence saved them; in His love and in His mercy He redeemed them, and He lifted them and carried them all the days of old." (Isaiah 63:9 NASB) Let me challenge you to apply this passage to your own situation and believe that when you suffer pain, in a mysterious yet very real way, Jesus feels it too.

If Jesus is the Head and we're His body, wouldn't He feel what we feel? The truth is He is carrying you. You have felt alone but you are not. He has been carrying you all along and will bring you home safely to ultimate healing. It's the truth of His presence with us and under us and in us and around us that truly saves us. Believe it—it's true. "Trust in the Lord with all your heart and do not lean on your own understanding. In all your ways acknowledge Him and He will make your paths straight." (Proverbs 3:5-6)

Job was a godly man. He loved God and followed His ways. God even bragged about him to Satan in heaven. God tested Job's faith using Satan as an afflicting agent. But there were boundaries across which Satan could not cross. God was in complete control. Job did not know of the heavenly wager. We do. We can see from a distance some of what God was doing, but not everything. What about the other angels looking on? What about the faith of Job's wife? Why did God allow Job's children to die? How did Job's sufferings develop the faith of Job's friends, etc.? We can surmise, but not fully comprehend.

Isn't it amazing that after the first two chapters of Job, the next 35 chapters consist of five men debating "Why?" Most of these chapters reveal Job's dialogue: lamenting, suffering, trying to understand and desperately seeking answers to his trial from God. Then God answers Job, but sovereignly accomplishes something far greater than merely answering "Why?" God turns the table and demands that Job answer Him, "Now gird up your loins like a man, and I will ask you and you will instruct me." (Job 38:3) Then, God gives Job a simple science test about things all around him in the natural world. Job can't answer any of God's questions. Afterward, Job answers the Lord, "Behold, I am insignificant; what can I reply to you? I lay my hand on my mouth." (Job 40:3-4) Up to this point, Job had leaned on his own understanding, which was woefully lacking.

Let me add here that God wants us to be reverently honest with Him. Pour out your heart to God—tell Him everything, cry out, tell Him how you feel, but do it with reverence as Job did. Honor God as God and pour out to Him the anguish of your soul's questions and concerns. He requires truth in the inward parts. Some of us are afraid to let it all out and others dishonor God in a defiant way. Don't choose either of those paths.[10] "Therefore, I will not restrain my mouth; I will speak in the anguish of my spirit; I will complain in the bitterness of my soul." (Job 7:11)

Then, in chapter 42, we discover what God has been waiting for and doing all along. The major issue or question on suffering is not "Why?" or "Who caused my suffering?" Rather, the major issue is Job's relationship with God. So, God zeroed in on Job. "Then Job answered the Lord and said, 'I know that you can do all things, and no purpose of Yours can be thwarted. I have heard of You by the hearing of the ear; but now my eye sees You; therefore, I retract and I repent in dust and ashes.'" (Job 42:1-2, 5-6)

"I heard things, but now I see you." God turned this whole ordeal into an opportunity to draw Job closer to Himself than he'd ever been. God's purposes were good and holy. God used Satan as His pawn, not vice-versa. Jesus said, "Blessed are the pure in heart for they shall see God." Are you and I seeing God clearly with the eye of faith? One day soon, we shall see Him with new eyes. This terrible adversity helped Job repent and see God as never before. *There's no greater payoff for adversity than to draw near to God and see His face, knowing that all things are made right between us.*

Following his conversation with the Lord, Job prayed for his friends. And God blessed Job's end more than his beginning. His family returned and "consoled and comforted him for all the adversities that the Lord had brought on him." (Job 42:11)

If you are a follower of Jesus Christ, God *will* test your faith and He often uses adversity. Job told his dear wife, "Shall we indeed accept good from God and not accept adversity." (Job 2:10) If we would truly look into the face of God, knowing who He really is, why would we not accept adversity from His hand? Can we lay the "Why?" in His hand and trust Him? You say, "If only I could see God!"—but you have—in the face of Jesus.

Chapter 4.
The Mysteries of Life

"Man's steps are ordained by the Lord, how then can man understand his way?" (Proverbs 20:24) Sir Winston Churchill expressed life as, "a riddle wrapped in a mystery inside an enigma."[11]

Much of life is a mystery. It's like showing up half-way through a highly technical lecture, about which we know little or nothing. I remember as a young man sitting in a graduation ceremony listening to a professor speak for an hour. I can honestly say that although I tried to understand what he was saying, ultimately I had no clue what he was talking about.

The psalmist, Asaph, contemplating a difficult situation, said, "When I tried to understand all this it was oppressive to me; till I entered the sanctuary of God; then I understood." (Psalm 73:16 NIV) Again, as we look to God and His Word, much is made clear—in fact more than we at first realize. Yet, in life's mysteries, leaning on our own understanding, trying to figure it all out can be oppressive.

Struggling to understand our suffering can consume, exhaust and drain us physically, mentally and emotionally. It can also run us down spiritually. Yet, like the psalmist, if we go into the presence of God and contemplate Him (i.e., "enter His sanctuary") a divine peace and wisdom begin to appear. Why? Because at the end of the day, like Job, what we really need is not all of life's answers, but *God Himself.* We need to know personally and trust explicitly the only *One* who has all the answers.

Could it be that *this* is really the bottom line of faith?—leaving the enigmas of life to God and exercising a gut-level trust in our faithful Creator and Savior, trusting Him in silence and being satisfied that having Him is enough?

Must we really first understand the entire layout of a large city in order to follow a simple map to our destination? And if our very steps are ordained by God (and they are) how in the world could we understand the totality of our lives from where we stand?

Paul told Timothy, "All Scripture is given by inspiration of God and is profitable for doctrine, for reproof, for correction, for instruction in righteousness that the man of God may be complete, thoroughly equipped for every good work." (2 Timothy 3:16-17 NKJV)

The only way we can know God is through His revelation of Himself to us. The Bible gives us everything we *need* to know about life and God. Does that mean, though, that there are other things about God and even life that we haven't been told? Yes. We are responsible for what we have been told. The rest we must trust to God. Is that an unreasonable requirement? Shouldn't we trust God with the unknowns, the things He is silent about?

That's why Paul could say, "I may be perplexed but I'm not in despair." (2 Corinthians 4:8) In fact, for God to be God there has to be infinite things He knows that we don't know. But what we do know about Him, through what He has revealed and what we've experienced of Him, is that He is good and faithful. So, we can trust Him for the conundrums of life.

Because something is mysterious or concealed from me, doesn't negate God's love for me. For instance, most people I have asked don't want to know in advance either the day of their death or how they will die. I don't have to understand all of the science behind light in order to enjoy the sun. Similarly, much of what's under the hood of my car baffles me and I'm glad for a trained mechanic. So, why not content ourselves to know that God knows what we cannot know? Again, is that enough for you and me?

During the times of Israel's judges, when Israel was particularly oppressed by enemies, the angel of the Lord approached Gideon and said something that threw him off balance. "'The Lord is with you, O valiant warrior.' Then Gideon said to him, 'O my Lord, if the Lord is with us, why then has all this happened to us? And where are all His miracles?'" (Judges 6:12-13)

Do you ever feel that way? "If God is with me (and I know from Scripture He dwells within me by His Spirit) then why am I experiencing such suffering?" "Lord, I need answers and I need a miracle—in fact, I need a bunch of miracles!"

The context of Judges, chapter six, explains *why* Gideon and Israel were experiencing such hardship. Israel had done evil in God's sight, so He gave them over to their enemies, the Midianites, for seven years. As in this case with Israel, sometimes we are told the "whys." Yet in the midst of Israel's struggles due to their own sin, Gideon finds favor with God: "The Lord is with you, O valiant warrior."

As God's children, we too have found favor with Him. Like Gideon, God says to us, "The Lord is with you, O valiant warrior." Do you see yourself as a valiant warrior in God's presence? You are. But you say: "I don't feel like one. I feel weak, insignificant and beat up." Paul reminds us in Romans 8:31 of the same truth, "If God is for us, [and He is!] who can be against us?" (See Romans 8:31-39.)

God is for us—Jesus gave us Himself—He gives us everything else we need. We are saved and Jesus prays for our victory. His love is stuck to us like superglue. No trial on earth, not even death itself can separate us from Him. "But in all these things, we overwhelmingly conquer through Him who loved us." O valiant warrior, know your God. Know His love.

I learned this valuable truth by a little note I found one morning that my loving wife, Denese, wrote me:

> Good morning, my brave and mighty warrior! "[What, what would have become of me] had I not believed [that I would] see the Lord's goodness in the land of the living! Wait and hope for and expect the Lord; be brave and of good courage, and let your heart be stout and enduring. Yes, wait and hope for and expect the Lord." (Psalm 27:13,14 The Amplified Bible) You are His anointed and He is your unyielding strength, Mark. He will never, no never leave us or forsake us. He is not slack concerning His promises—they are YES! Today, and forever, I love you with all my heart. D. XOXOXO (Hugs and kisses)

When I got up that morning I did not feel like a mighty warrior. I felt mighty weak and insignificant. After reading this, I sensed a renewed strength because of who the Lord has declared us to be. Who will we believe—our feelings or our Lord?

About a year ago, we had a friend over, who is single and has never been married. He's in his late 50's. I could tell he felt low and somewhat beat up from life. I was led of the Lord to reaffirm him in the Lord. I told him, "I've known you for 30 years and you have always sought the Lord—yes, you've had your ups and downs, we all have, but here today you are still a man of faith seeking your God." Tears welled up in his eyes. He said, "You don't know how much that means to me." Maybe he had no one for years to just tell him "You're doing OK." You, mighty warrior! Go in the Lord's strength!

It's okay to ask, "Why?" Jesus did. (Matthew 27:46) When reason is lacking or when reason just isn't enough—God is enough! As Corrie ten Boom would say: "Look around and be distressed—Look within and be depressed—Look to Jesus and be at rest."

After all, at the end of each day it's not about us; it's about Jesus. "It's in Christ that we find out who we are and what we are living for. Long before we first heard of Christ and got our hopes up, He had His eye on us, had designs on us for glorious living, part of the overall purpose He is working out in everything and everyone." (Ephesians 1:11-12 MSG) Do you believe that?

Let me end this chapter with another quote. "Have you ever come upon anything quite like this extravagant generosity of God, this deep, deep wisdom? It's way over our heads. We'll never figure it out. Is there anyone around who can explain God?—Anyone smart enough to tell Him what to do?—Anyone who has done Him such a huge favor that God has to ask his advice? Everything comes from Him; everything happens through Him; everything ends up in Him. ALWAYS GLORY! ALWAYS PRAISE! Yes. Yes. Yes." (Romans 11:33-36 MSG)

Maybe the real mystery is: Why don't we trust this God?

Chapter 5.
Go Back to What You Know

"Christ is the aperture through which the immensity and magnificence of God can be seen."[12]

As a fellow-sufferer, may I share some thoughts with you that have helped me on my life's journey? I know our trials look different, but we all struggle with the same basic questions and needs in terms of our suffering. I'm not saying that I can begin to fully comprehend the pain, sorrow, grief, fear, or exhaustion you have experienced or are experiencing. None of us can fully live in another's shoes.

We also must be careful not to simply compare trials. Someone may experience more pain than you, but it's not *your* pain. Your pain is what you know. It's not wise to compare trials. Dr. Jerry Sitser comments on this. He lost three generations of his family in one car accident—his mother, his wife, and his daughter. As incredibly painful as that was, Dr. Sitser wonders whether his pain is any worse than that of a wife whose spouse requires nursing care for many years in their home. As he says, such comparisons are fruitless. Each of us must carry the burden of life we are given. *The really important issue is whether we push God away in our suffering, or run toward Him.*

In order to give you a window of insight into my suffering let me describe it here briefly for you. I was born with a rare bone disease that required surgery. In that surgery, I developed hepatitis from the anesthetic that nearly took my life. Meanwhile, my wife had to deal with two children under two years and the prospect of losing her young husband.

My suffering also includes being sexually abused as a teenager by a medical doctor. I was too ashamed and frightened to tell my parents. I've endured numerous kidney stones, two of which hospitalized me for ten days.

In addition to the above, I've suffered a hard-to-diagnose, chronic pain syndrome for the past 15 years. The doctors are bewildered by what may have caused it and they have only guesses on how to treat it. As a result of my illness, our finances have been depleted and I've had to step away from a career that I love. All of this has spawned loneliness, anguish, isolation and misunderstanding. The pain of all this has been very real to me, as I know your pain is very real to you. So what do we do? How do we journey through it? What's the answer?

Dear friend, we don't know all the *whys*. We all have questions: "If God is all-powerful why doesn't He stop this madness?" "Isn't there some other way?" "Why do the innocent suffer?" "Does God really care?"

I too have asked and struggled with these and many other questions. Thankfully, God's Word answers many of them. Yet, on our journey of faith, it seems many questions will remain unanswered. There is a mystery to God's ways and dealings with us as we saw in the previous chapter. He is an infinite, all knowing God and we are not. We are finite and pathetically limited in our over-all knowledge. So, what do we do? How do we process the unknowns and perplexities?

The answer is: *We go back to what we know!* And what do we know? What has God clearly told us? What bed-rock truths can we turn to, stand on, count on and always know for certain? What is there in life that is unquestionable and absolute that can give us a firm foothold and handhold? Where do we find a vantage point from which we can see the bigger picture and find meaning and hope?

We must go back to what we know! We must go back to the God who knows and has revealed Himself to us. Dear friend, this has been my salvation. This is what gets me through day after day when nothing else seems to change and the suffering continues.

As I focus on God and what He wants me to know, a lot begins to make sense. What do we know?

- We know God loves me and cares about me more than we can imagine! How do we know? Because of Jesus! God, the Father, proved He loves us by providing His Son, Jesus. "But God demonstrates His own love toward us, in that while we were still sinners, Christ died for us." (Romans 5:8) So, no matter what circumstances are screaming at us, one thing we know and never have to wonder—God loves us and proved it by sacrificing His Son for us.

- We know God is for us! He wants us to win; to be victorious. Even though circumstances assault us and cause us to think God is against us, the actual truth is: "What then shall we say to these things?

If God is for us who can be against us?" (Romans 8:31)

- We know God will always take care of us! "And my God shall supply all your needs according to His riches in glory by Christ Jesus." (Philippians 4:19) The Amplified Bible expands this thought beautifully in Hebrews 13:5, "For He, God Himself, has said, I will not in any way fail you nor give you up nor leave you without support. I will not. I will not. I will not in any degree leave you helpless nor forsake nor let you down [relax my hold on you]. Assuredly not!" Do you believe that? Go back now and re-read that slowly. How serious is God about you? Write it in the front of your Bible and read it often. I have and I do and it has changed my life.

I know my trials and suffering will someday end. "But, may the God of all grace, who called us to eternal glory by Christ Jesus, *after* you have suffered a *while*, perfect, establish, strengthen and settle you." (1 Peter 5:10) Right now the pain never seems to end, but it will. God will personally see to it.

Our suffering has purpose and meaning because we are a part of a much bigger redemptive story. The prophetic Scriptures remind us of God's intended end for our tears, affliction, suffering, persecution and pain. There is a new day coming in Heaven. Be encouraged about your future and in the mean time, God is perfecting our faith and character—two very important things to God.

So, dear friend, know that one overruling activity God is performing in your life, is to transform you from the inside out and prepare you for your heavenly home with Jesus. We must never underestimate that activity of God in our lives or its importance. As Max Lucado aptly says, "God loves you just the way you are, but He *refuses* to leave you that way. He wants you to be just like Jesus."[13]

Why does He refuse to leave us in our old sinful ways? Because we have underestimated sin and its destructive ways. But Jesus loves us too much to leave us in that condition. So, though He loves us while we're in that condition, He refuses to leave us there. And as we sometimes underestimate sin, so we underestimate His love and grace. We need to know this and then experience it by submission, surrender and yieldedness to His loving transformation.

Let's linger here a moment, because knowing that Christ intends to transform us is critical to following Him. Upon placing my faith and trust in Jesus for my salvation, He places me in a favorable relationship with Himself and places His Spirit in me. This Holy Spirit of God, the Spirit of grace and truth, is lovingly relentless to transform my character into the very image of Christ. Actually, to say that He is *relentless* is a massive understatement! God will do whatever it takes, using any creative trial as deep or as hard as it may be in order to transform us.

Our trials and suffering in this life cannot be compared with the glory we will share and experience when we see God face to face (2 Corinthians 4:17). You see, without holiness, no one will see the Lord (Hebrews 12:14). We must be transformed into the very character of Christ—love, joy, peace, patience, kindness, goodness, faithfulness, gentleness and self-control— this is for God's glory and our ultimate good.

At some point in our faith walk with God, you and I must come to a place of ongoing rest and trust in our faithful God to work in us, using any means He deems best. Paul says it well, "For we don't want you to be unaware, brothers, of our affliction that took place in the province of Asia; we were *completely overwhelmed—beyond our strength*—so that we even despaired of life. However, we personally had a death sentence within ourselves, so that we would not trust in ourselves, but in God, who raises the dead." (2 Corinthians 1:8,9 HCSB)

Dear friend, your trial may seem strange. Perhaps you feel completely overwhelmed, beyond your own strength. The good thing is that you are right where God wants you—in a place of resurrection, a place of new life—of gut-level, life-and-death trust in the Great Faithful One. He has delivered you in the past, He is delivering you presently, and He will yet deliver you. Your soul has "entered the iron." You have come to the end of yourself. You have no strength left.

You may have heard people say, "God never lays on you more than you can handle." Yet, your experience cries out, "Not so!" Paul knows how you feel. You have been taken beyond your ability that you might know the mystery and power of a resurrected life and faith. Jesus said, "I am the resurrection and the life." Are we experiencing Jesus this moment—His life, His strength, His joy? Your soul is in incredible anguish, but this trial will end. Its purpose of growing your valuable faith will conclude and you will be gloriously delivered into the presence of Jesus, forever healed, forever free, forever fully alive.

So, in your anguish now, cry to Jesus. Your tears are precious to Him. He "captures every tear and keeps them in a bottle." (Psalm 56:8) He feels your pain and has a glorious end in mind.

What else do we know?

- We know that in our relationship with Jesus, He has given us a place to stand and a reason to rejoice. "Through (Jesus) we have access by faith into this grace in which we stand and rejoice in hope of the glory of God." (Romans 5:2) Again, when our lives seem to be falling apart and crumbling all around us, we have a rock-solid, wide, secure place to take our stand—the grace place—Jesus Himself. That is reason enough to rejoice.

- We know that humbling circumstances give us an unexpected blessing. "God resists the proud but gives grace to the humble." (1 Peter 5:5) The more humble we are and submissive to God the more grace we receive.

- We know we have nothing to fear. "Fear not for I am with you; be not dismayed, for I am your God. I will strengthen you, yes I will help you. I will uphold you with my righteous right hand." (Isaiah 41:10) When someone goes through a chronic trial, fears come automatically. This is human. And yet fears can overwhelm us. We can experience anxiety and panic attacks that can be debilitating. Paul reminded Timothy: "For God has not given us a spirit of fearfulness, but one of power, love and sound judgement." (2 Timothy 1:7 HCSB) In other words, the fear is human, but the Holy Spirit that is given to us to help us is the Spirit of power, love and a sound mind to overcome these debilitating fears. This is something very important to know and believe. The Psalms as well as the entire Bible have so much to say about our fearfulness. There are many great and precious promises. The great antidote to fear is faith—believing the promises of God and embracing His presence.

- We know there is no one and nothing else we can turn to for help, but God. "I, even I, am the Lord, and besides me there is no Savior." (Isaiah 43:11) One time, after some people stopped following Jesus, Jesus turned to Peter and said, "Will you leave too? And Peter answered: 'Where else can I go—you alone have the words of eternal life.'" (John 6:68)

What other alternative do we have? Jesus is our only hope. Sin, suffering and death came into this world through Adam's sin. Sin opened Pandora's Box. The bigger picture of suffering is the ugly presence of sin—either mine or someone else's. Could God stop it? Of course! Will He? Very soon. He promises to return soon and make all things right. But until then there is a period in human history of suffering. This is allowed by the wisdom of God and not totally understood by us. But we do know that suffering provides both a *test* of our faith to demonstrate our genuine trust in God and a *means* for transforming and preparing us for eternity.

Our God is the Most High God. The buck stops with Him. There is no other God or Savior. There is no one else to turn to. The cross of Jesus is the center point of human history and God's redemptive story. The attributes of God, the mystery of God, the great plan of God are all laser-focused through Jesus at the cross. And just like that day was promised and came, so His Second Coming is promised and will soon come and make all things right. During this time of mystery, hurt, pain and sin we must trust Him. "So those who suffer according to God's will, should, in doing good, entrust themselves to a faithful creator." (1 Peter 4:19 HCSB)

God is a faithful Creator and very loving Savior. He is worthy of our love and trust. So, though His ways are not always understood by us, His character must be. We must come back to what He has revealed to us about Him. We must lean all our weight and understanding on what we do know—the Person and promises of God Himself.

Sometimes, in response to our prayers and faith, God delivers us *from* a dreadful situation, but often He delivers us *through* it. But again, we know that He walks through our pain with us, right through to the other side. The timing and means of deliverance are up to Him.

I end this chapter with a challenge for you to get in the Scriptures and begin to write down truths God has revealed to us. Things about God we can know for sure. I am listing some below to help you get started. *Go back to what you know!*

WE KNOW:

- God is good and righteous
- Though He may seem silent, He is always present
- He can be trusted
- He is unchanging
- He is faithful
- He works from an eternal perspective
- God is not surprised by our trials—He designed them
- Each trial comes through God, and therefore brings great purpose
- Hope is an anchor for the soul. We hope in God
- God's mercies are new every morning
- We can daily choose to rejoice in the Lord
- When we are weak, He is strong
- He seeks to make us holy

- He prunes us to produce more fruit
- It's always fitting to praise Jesus
- In everything to give thanks
- God is up to something special when He sends difficulty our way
- Life is hard, but God is good
- God is sovereignly providential over every detail of life
- We are pilgrims on a journey
- Trials are temporary
- God owns everything, controls everything, provides everything
- To live one day at a time, one moment at a time
- Jesus is not only the destination, but the way to it
- God takes us much further than we think possible
- Never underestimate sin
- God works for good in our lives
- God's Spirit abides in us
- We are united to Christ by faith
- God's ways are much higher than our ways
- Jesus' yoke is easy and His burden is light
- We fight from a position of victory
- The just shall live by faith
- Our sins are forgiven in Christ
- The joy of the Lord is our strength
- Jesus is coming very soon
- He will never leave us or forsake us
- Nothing can separate us from God's love
- Suffering is a calling from God
- The cross of Jesus gives us true perspective
- Through the cross God says to us: I care, I feel your pain, I am near, I personally share your anguish. I stand by to help, to love, to take you to Myself
- He must increase but we must decrease

The greatest mistake is to think God doesn't care.

"He did not even spare His own Son, but offered Him up for us all; how will He not also with Him grant us everything." (Romans 8:32)

Go back to what you know!

Chapter 6.
What am I Waiting for?

"We are so afraid of silence that we chase ourselves from one event to the next in order not to spend a moment alone with ourselves, in order not to have to look at ourselves in the mirror."[14]

Our American culture seems to demand of us: "Don't just stand there; do something." Sometimes the culture of faith also beckons us to step out into action. But an often neglected balance to this is: "Don't just do something; stand there." The psalmist reminds us "Be still and know that I am God." (Psalm 46:10) No other verse has encouraged me more, in my journey through adversity.

For the chronic sufferer, *waiting* is not usually a choice. We're thrust into it. We're asked to sit in the waiting room of life. Chronic trials often reduce our activities to a bare minimum. We just don't have the energy reserves to do much more than survive the day.

Along with waiting comes, what many Christian writers express as "the dark night of the soul." These are times in our life when we are waiting on God, but He seems silent. Certain trials seem to lead us into a forced solitude. We know clearly from many Scriptures that God's Spirit will not leave or forsake us, but there is a soul perception of a *dark solitude*. The psalmist asks, "Why are you downcast, O my soul?" (Psalm 42:43)

In Genesis 15 when God was "cutting" a covenant with Abraham, verse 12 explains, "As the sun was setting, Abram fell into a deep sleep and a thick and dreadful darkness came over him." The Lord goes on to prophesy that Abram's descendants would "be enslaved and mistreated four hundred years," then afterward they would be delivered and possess great riches. Then verse 17 says, "When the sun had set and darkness had fallen, a smoking firepot, with a blazing torch appeared...." (NIV)

Out of the darkness God made His great covenant with Abram, who is the Father of faith. "The scriptures foresaw that God would justify the Gentiles by faith, and announced the Gospel, in advance, to Abraham: *'All nations will be blessed through you.'* So, those who have faith are blessed along with Abraham, the man of faith." (Galatians 3:8-9)

As Joseph sat in the prison with irons on his feet and around his neck, confined and alone, he experienced the dark night of the soul—his soul entered the iron.

Even on the cross, I believe, Jesus experienced this dark night of the soul as He took on the sin of the world, "From the sixth hour until the ninth hour darkness came over all the land. About the ninth hour Jesus cried out in a loud voice, 'Eloi, Eloi, lama sabachthani?'—which means, 'My God, my God, why have you forsaken me?'" (Matthew 27:45,46 NIV) Because the Father had laid on Jesus the sin of the world, including mine, at that moment God the Father forsook His own Son. Jesus experienced the full outpouring of God's wrath against sin as our sin-bearer.

So how does this now relate to us in those times when God seems distant and silent, when the way seems very dark?

First, we go back to what we know—that Jesus took our sin and exchanged if for His righteousness. "God made Him who had no sin to be sin for us, so that in Him we might become the righteousness of God." (2 Corinthians 5:21 NIV) Second, we know He will never leave us or remove us from His love. Third, because we still live in a sin-soaked world, where the enemy seeks to steal, kill, and destroy, the spiritual battle rages. Our faith is being tested and built up.

The prophet Isaiah gives us insight here. God tells us: "I am the Lord, and there is no other. I form the light and create darkness; I bring prosperity and create disaster; I, the Lord, do these things." (Isaiah 45:6-7) In that chapter we have a prophecy 150 years in advance of its fulfillment, telling of the Persian king, Cyrus, who would assist the Jews in returning to their land after 70 years of captivity. Among other things God wanted Cyrus to know, God was providentially going to give him victory in conquests. The Jewish historian Josephus cites that Isaiah influenced Cyrus with this prophecy.[15]

The prophet Jeremiah also spoke of this. (Ezra 1:1-11) God did stir up Cyrus to build a new temple in Jerusalem for the worship of God and Cyrus knew it. The Persians had been the Jew's captors, but now they helped them return to worship God in their own land.

What I want us to see is, "I will give you the treasures of darkness, riches stored in secret places, so that you may know that I am the Lord, the God of Israel, who summons you by name." (Isaiah 45:3) This was a word to Cyrus, but it was read by the Jews and is applicable to us as well. The 70 years of captivity were a very dark but necessary time of cleansing for Israel. God was sovereignly overseeing it and brought them through the darkness to the other side. Within this darkness were treasures: treasures of cleansing—no more idols; treasures of insights and hope—the great prophecies of world history in Daniel were given; the treasures of faithfulness—seeing God provide, protect and patiently wait. Yes, the Lord waits for us just as we wait on Him.

I believe there are treasures that can only be found in the *darkness of suffering*. These treasures are what we're waiting for. In our suffering, let us mine for the treasures of faith God wants to give us. In the darkness of loneliness, silence, and confinement, let the darkness of God perform its work. David, a chronic sufferer at the hands of Saul, cried out, "If I say, 'Surely the darkness will hide me and the light become night around me,' even the darkness will not be dark to you; the night will shine like the day, for darkness is as light to you." (Psalm 139:11-12 NIV) Above all, know that our treasure is actually Jesus. We have a transformed heart in fellowship with the Treasure of all Treasures! Paul wrote to the Colossians, "Christ, in whom are hidden all the treasures of wisdom and knowledge." (Colossians 2:2-3 NIV) Paul prayed:

> For this reason, since the day we heard about you, we have not stopped praying for you and asking God to fill you with the knowledge of His will through all spiritual wisdom and understanding. And we pray this in order that you may live a life worthy of the Lord and may please Him in every way: bearing fruit in every good work, growing in the knowledge of God, being strengthened with all power according to His glorious might, so that you may have *great endurance and patience,* and *joyfully giving thanks* to the *Father,* who has qualified you to *share in* the inheritance of the saints in the *kingdom of light.* For He has *rescued us* from the *dominion of darkness* and *brought us* into the *kingdom of the Son* he loves,

in whom we have redemption, the forgiveness of sins."
(Colossians 1:9-14 NIV)

Remember that though a cloud of darkness may blow over us, Jesus has already delivered us from the territory and dominion of darkness. Let the darkness crowd you to Jesus. Maybe the loneliness and silence is meant as a privilege to enable us to see the depths of His love for us; as a means of emptying us so He might fill us. The great exchange: Our sin for His righteousness—Our pain for His glory—Our loneliness for His presence—Our loss for His filling—Our dying for His life. Is it worth the exchange for you?

I have discussed this "dark night of the soul" in the context of waiting on God, because it seems that the dark night of the soul always occurs during times of waiting. But what does it mean to "wait on the Lord?" Waiting on the Lord does not mean passive laziness, apathy, or hopeless impatience. We might say there are two main types waiting on God:

1. One type of waiting is what a waiter does in a restaurant. Three of my children have worked as waiters, and I can tell you, it's a tough job. Waiters work hard. They are vigilant and attentive to the needs of those they serve. They avoid distractions and focus on their tables. They are detailed and walk a lot. Without being a nuisance, they stand back and watch for needs and try to anticipate. They take the heat from the kitchen. Waiters are actively waiting. This is how much of our lives are lived in active service.

2. A second form of waiting, spoken of much in Scripture has to do with "Don't just do something, stand there!" Time elapses slowly. You want to

> jump ahead and fix things and God says, "Wait".
> This waiting is active, doing the daily things we're
> all called to do like Joseph. This waiting has more
> to do with patience and *long*-suffering. This is the
> type of waiting I want to focus on in the rest of this
> chapter.

After the fall of Jerusalem, and during the dark night of Israel waiting on God's 70-year discipline, Jeremiah wrote the Lamentations. Jeremiah despairs, "I remember my affliction and my wandering, the bitterness and the gall. I well remember them, and my soul is downcast within me." (Lamentations 3:19-20 NIV) We feel that way at times. Even though we may know we didn't cause our trial, we have a general sense of guilt anyway. Jeremiah didn't directly cause Israel's downfall—he preached for repentance. But he too was an Israelite, and by association shared their guilt and pain. In the darkness of despair, Jeremiah mines a jewel, a treasure of hope:

> Yet, this I call to mind and therefore I have hope; be-
> cause of the Lord's great love, we are not consumed, for
> His compassions never fail. They are new every morning;
> great is your faithfulness. I say to myself, *"The Lord is my
> portion; therefore I will wait for Him"* The Lord is good to
> those whose hope is in Him, to the one who seeks Him;
> it is *good* to *wait quietly* for the salvation of the Lord. It is
> good for a man to bear the yoke while he is young. Let
> him sit alone in silence for the Lord has laid it on him.
> (Lamentations 3:21-28 NIV)

What are some lessons with which we can summarize this chapter?

1.   Hope is vital. But like faith, the object of hope must be the Lord.

2. Keep in mind God's great, merciful, love.

3. The only reason we're not consumed is because of His activity of compassion.

4. Every day has a fresh batch of mercy and love.

5. We have totally underestimated God's faithfulness to us, especially in trials. His faithfulness is GREAT!

6. What am I *waiting* for?—Something to change? No, I'm waiting for the Lord and Him alone. "The Lord acts on behalf of the one who waits for Him." (Isaiah 64:4) While we're waiting, God is acting— He's at work all around us and in us.

7. Like hope, my expectations must be in God. "My soul, wait silently for God alone, for my expectation is from Him." (Psalm 62:5) Is this true for us? Someone has said that the worst depressions come from unfulfilled expectations. It's true, our expectations take a hit by adversity. They become vacuums of loss, black holes sucking out our life. There are many losses: job, health, spouse, child, friend, church, dreams, careers, etc. But my greatest expectation must be God—we must allow Him to fill the void, not with what we think should happen or understand to take place to fix things, but literally expect God to be God in our situation. Embrace Him, His promises, and His mysteries and His timing.

8. It is a good thing to wait on God. Waiting is not bad—yes, hard, at times—but good, beneficial, helpful, favorable.

9. Seek Him while you wait. Don't wait in the vacuum. Let Him rush in. You also rush to Him. Seek Him through love, study, prayer, etc.

10. Learn lessons early in life as they come. If you are called as a young person to wait—you are privileged.

11. God lays the yoke of waiting on us. He initiates it. The first words my brother Daniel ever said were

actually a sentence. "Let's have a little cooperation around here!" He had heard Mom say that to
us five rascals a few times. But isn't that what God
is saying? Let's cooperate with Him while we wait.

12.   Wait quietly or even silently. Like the psalmist prayed—Lord, set a watch over my mouth.
Be careful of irreverence or complaining to others. Yes, pour out your heart to God, but watch
what you say in haste or frustration. In the midst
of suffering, the hard legalistic edges are often smoothed out by the file of grace. We often
change our dogmatic views about much that is
non-essential. Maybe, through quiet waiting, we
can listen to God's voice better too. Someone
said, "If you wallow in self-pity, then the pictures
of pain will become mirrors, and all you'll see is
yourself."

Waiting on God, especially in a time of suffering, is hard.
But it is the way of God. Waiting is how our faith and trust are
developed. When all the props are kicked out and there is
nothing left, will I keep waiting? This then begs the question:
"How long must I wait…for my son to come back to the Lord…
for my health to return…for a job…for the pain to go away?"
The only answer I can see that has any value and meaning is,
"Until God says, 'Enough.'" Will that be in this life or the next?
Only God knows. Will you trust Him for the duration? You see,
God doesn't have to answer. He simply is the answer! Faith says
that is okay! That is enough for me!

Watchman Nee observed, "We like to be always 'on the
go': the Lord would sometimes prefer to have us in prison,
we think, in terms of Apostolic journeys; God dares to put His
greatest ambassadors in chains."[16] Charles Spurgeon assert-

ed, "I have a great need for Christ; I have a great Christ for my need."[17]

To wait on God is to believe with expectation. Waiting on Him is not apathetic resignation. Neither should we assume that He will just do what we want, but He will show Himself strong on our behalf. Waiting means to be attentive to God. Waiting means to be pliable to the Potter. Waiting means to get up in the morning and report to Him for duty. Waiting means looking daily for God to reveal Himself to you. Waiting is an attitude of brokenness and surrender that quiets our fretting soul in the arms of a loving God. Waiting quiets the soul to hear the heartbeat of God. Waiting is the heart cry of Glory to God in the Highest. Waiting is the place where He increases and we decrease. Waiting on God is stepping into harmony with His waiting for us.

So let us wait all day long, continually, as a calling. Wait dependently on the Holy Spirit: expectantly, earnestly, silently, patiently, restfully, confidently, and obediently. Know that God will come and make all things right in His time.

Wait for guidance, protection, strength, consolation, and salvation, and wait for a word from God and write it down. Wait with resolve and prayer. Wait for God's opportunities. Understand that waiting is the exercise of the soul. Use it to establish your heart. Jesus is waiting for the subduing of all His enemies—wait here with Him.

Those who wait on God are:
- Heard by God
- Shown grace
- Blessed

Those who wait on God:
- Experience goodness
- Learn contentment and patience
- Are unashamed and
- Will inherit the earth

When you are asked to wait in the dark night storm, be still and know your God. In Christ, speak peace to your heart. Know that He cares about you. He has not abandoned you. In fact, He is entrusting you with the silence.

Tony Evans recounts this story:

One day a young boy was on an airplane flight when the plane got caught in a storm and hit some very bad turbulence. The plane was rocking back and forth, and trays were sliding around. People were getting scared and some began to scream as the plane pitched back and forth and dipped up and down.

But in the middle of all this chaos, the boy just kept on playing. When the plane dipped, he said, "Wheeeeee!" while everyone else was screaming.

A little old lady sitting next to the boy asked him, "Son, how can you play and be happy at a time like this?"

The boy looked at her and said, "Oh, it's easy. My daddy's the pilot."[18]

Once you know Jesus is in charge, your perspective changes.

As a fellow *waiter* may I give you a tip? "Wait on the Lord; be of good courage and He shall strengthen your heart; wait I say, on the Lord!" (Psalm 27:4 NKJV)

Chapter 7.
Be a Believing Believer

"For all times and conditions, faith in the God of deliverance is the secret of triumph in the Christian life. FAITH IS: resting in His love, His presence, His provision."[19]

One of the things that always bothered me about the story of Joseph and it's relation to me personally was his divine dreams prior to his suffering. We're told that when Joseph was 17 years old he was tending sheep with his brothers. Joseph was apparently loved by his dad, Jacob, more than the other boys and they knew it. The special coat of many colors Jacob gave to Joseph served as a visible symbol of Jacob's favoritism toward him. To add fuel to their hatred of this favoritism, Joe tattled on them. The last straw, however, was his dreams, in which Joseph saw himself reigning over his brothers. And young Joseph didn't have the sense to keep his dreams to himself, but shared them openly with his brothers. Though these prophetic dreams made the boys jealous with hatred, Jacob knew there was something to them (see Genesis 37).

Joseph's dreams were different than a lot of our dreams. We often confuse God's dream for us with simply the American Dream. As a kid I dreamed of being a successful major league baseball player. We have dreams of careers, homes, family, travel, cars, sports and hobbies, etc. But Joseph's dreams were given to him by divine appointment and, though not fully understood, would become vital for him to "get through" the difficult years ahead. In this sense I think many believers can know even from childhood the dream God has for them. Yet, I never had a dream in the night when God showed me His plan for my life. So, what about the majority of us who didn't have a dream at the front end of our chronic trial? During the nights, in prison, I'm sure Joseph looked back on those dreams and was encouraged in his faith. What does our faith see?

At the top of God's "Most Important List" is our faith. "Without faith it is impossible to please God." (Hebrews 11:6) Faith (trust in Him) brings God great pleasure and consequently pleasure to us too. Faith can be seen and it sees the unseen. When the men lowered the crippled man down through the roof to be healed, Jesus "saw" their faith. It was very visible, very noticeable. Genuine faith displays itself simply in its own exercise. At the same time, genuine faith sees things not visible to the eyes. Faith can see the providence and love of God in a difficult situation. Faith can see unknown but real solutions to problems because God is seen to be present.

A case in point is found in the story of Elisha. In 2 Kings 6:15 NIV we read, "When the servant of the man of God got up and went out early the next morning, an army with horses and chariots had surrounded the city. 'Oh no, my lord! What shall we do?' the servant asked." Have you ever asked yourself or your spouse that? You are surrounded by troubles, which often happens in a chronic trial. The initial trial of suffering is bad enough, but then like weeds, additional trials begin to spring up everywhere. Perhaps you have become disabled or divorced and your finances take a hit, to put it mildly. The disability income isn't enough to live on and medical bills pile up. Your husband left you at home with the children with no job and no child-support. You're surrounded and overwhelmed.

Other weeds begin popping up, choking out your relationships. People don't understand your situation. Everyone seems to have pat answers. When you don't take their advice (because you can't or you've already tried) they reject you. Your church doesn't even understand. Rumors start, conclusions drawn. A spouse leaves. Children are frustrated. Tensions rise.

Then the weeds of mental and emotional struggles emerge. Your doctor has no answers so he/she tells you, "Your illness is all in your head." You begin to wonder whether it is. "Am I going crazy?" You get depressed and discouraged. The trial becomes overwhelming. You see yourself as simply a victim. Your emotions flare up: fears, anxieties, feelings of bitterness, loneliness, rejection. The cumulative effect is a deep soul anguish. Your soul is fusing with iron.

Among other things, and certainly not least, is the spiritual aspect of the trial. And we begin to question many things. Even some basic things like the reality of our faith: "Who exactly is God?" "Why don't our circumstances seem to align with His promises?" "Are we being punished for our sin?" "Is this a discipline for a deficiency?" Some people insist that if we had enough faith, we could escape all this.

Well, let's go back to the story in 2 Kings 6 and see how Elisha responded to his servant. "He said, 'Do not be afraid, for those who are with us are more than those who are with them.' Then Elisha prayed and said, 'O Lord, please open his eyes that he may see.' So, the Lord opened the eyes of the young man, and he saw, and behold, the mountain was full of horses and chariots of fire all around Elisha." (2 Kings 6:16-17) The chariots of fire were the angels of the Lord's army surrounding them to protect them. As you read on they were protected and victorious.

From this story in 2 Kings 6, let's glean a few truths:

1.   God is at work all around us even when our eyes can't see it.
2.   In the exercise of faith don't be afraid, but believe God. How many times in Scripture are we told not to be afraid? The antidote to fear is faith.
3.   When overwhelmed by trials, pray, "O Lord, please open my eyes that I may see what you are up to."
4.   Be encouraged. You are not alone.
5.   Remember, sometimes God delivers us *from* trials and sometimes *through* them. Either way requires faith.
6.   Faith opens our eyes to a whole new perspective.

The Amplified Bible tells us that faith is, "the conviction that God exists and is the Creator and Ruler of all things, the Provider and Bestower of eternal salvation through Christ, *(and)* the leaning of the entire human personality on God in absolute trust and confidence in His power, wisdom and goodness." (Hebrews 13:7 TAB) So, faith sees who God is and embraces His promises (starting with our salvation). Then when life hurls suffering at us and the darkness of the unknown prevents us from seeing the reasons why, *faith*, like a night vision scope, sees through the darkness and reveals the presence of God. Faith is believing *and leaning* on the person of Christ. In any situation we can lean one way or the other. We can lean to our own understanding which is incredibly myopic and puny (I can't even remember what I had for dinner last night!) or we can lean on God's character—His power, wisdom and goodness. Are we leaning fully and completely on God in absolute trust and confidence?

When we begin to see the invisible God by faith, He opens our eyes and brings peace and confidence. "You will keep him in perfect peace, whose mind is stayed on You, because he trusts in You." (Isaiah 26:3 NKJV) This trust magnifies God in the situation. Faith vision is on and operating and now our faith can be seen in tangible ways by others. We're calmer, more confident, and active in good works; our attitude can be seen to be grateful and thankful to God. We do things and say things that are in alignment with what we're seeing. And what we're seeing is not only that God is present, but in response to our trust in Him, He acts in favorable ways on our behalf. "Blessed is the man who makes the Lord his trust..." (Psalm 40:4)

Faith also knows that God doesn't always reveal His grand plan—He reveals Himself. Neither does faith deny the reality or intensity of my painful situation, but in the midst of that reality is a greater reality—the reality of God in my situation. Elisha didn't deny that the Syrian army was there, but he refocused attention on the greater reality—the truth of God's presence. I believe a deeper grasp of this truth can go a long way in helping us through our trial. We can often rehearse our trials in great detail, but can we rehearse God's greater truths and promises? Even more, do we believe them?

This was vividly illustrated at a rural church in south central Montana, where I had the privilege of serving as pastor for four-and-a-half years. In a relatively short period of time nearly every family in the church experienced tragedy, some still ongoing:

- One family's only son was brain-injured in a vehicle roll over. They have been through incredible things they never wanted and yet their faith is not only intact, but a trophy of grace on God's mantle. They have made the best of it and allowed God to do greater things than otherwise would have been done. They have been an inspiration to many. They are believing God for the greater reality of His presence.

- Another woman had a very serious accident shattering her leg. She trusted God and continues to serve the Lord.
- A man lost his elderly mother as she went out on the highway in front of her house to get the mail. A semi broad-sided her.
- Another very strong and hearty man woke up in the middle of the night with a seizure that was discovered to be cancer in numerous places. He never got angry or bitter, but continued to trust that God had a bigger plan.
- A friend at 50 years of age died suddenly one night.
- Another dear man nearly bled to death just down the hall from the emergency room. And there were other tragedies as well.

I share these stories because all of these families hurt deeply, but all of them kept looking to God. And their faith has proved genuine by their perseverance and thanks to God for deliverance, both in and through the trials.

Some trials result directly due to strained or broken relationships. Warren Wiersbe reminds us, "Be kind, for everyone you meet is fighting a battle."[20] So true. Some of these people we know; some we don't. If your trial stems from a damaged relationship, let Jesus come between you. Paul reminds us that "the only thing that counts is faith working through love." (Galatians 5:6)

A friend of ours from another church vividly displayed this faith working through love when her husband married another woman and then asked his estranged wife to live with them. She did not move in with them, but she embraced God's greater truth, the power of Jesus to forgive the unforgivable. She kept her heart free from bitterness, and entrusted her soul to her faithful Creator while continuing to do good. She eventually had the opportunity to lead her ex-husband's wife to Christ. Her motto is: *Life is hard, but God is good.* Without denying her pain, she is seeing the invisible.

Faith believes Jesus when He says: "My grace is sufficient for you, for my power is made perfect in weakness." (2 Corinthians 12:9) Faith is looking to God to change us instead of demanding He change our circumstances. Faith is believing we are victors, not victims. Were you sexually abused as a child? Were you raped as an adult? Today, as a believer, will you believe: "No, in all these things we are more than conquerors through him who loved us." (Romans 8:37)

I have a dear friend who was repeatedly abused by her father as a child. It took an unbelievable toll on her through the years. But later she became a follower of Christ and through the years learned to see by faith. As her father became older and an invalid, she took care of him and even bathed him. She forgave him and showed him the love of Christ. Just days before he died she and her husband had the privilege of leading him to a saving knowledge of Christ.

Faith perseveres and takes risks. I say "risk" because we associate stepping out and trusting God with risk. But let me take back the word "risk" because there is no risk in trusting God (as if there is a percentage of risk involved). Our only risk is in *not* trusting Him. And in not trusting God failure is guaranteed.

Has your trial continued for months now? How about 10 years? 30 years? Is your trial a no-end-in-sight, till-death-do-us-part trial? I quote again Pamela Reeve in her powerful little book *Faith Is:*

> Faith is:
> • Believing that the persevering, seemingly unanswered prayer of many years is not an exercise in futility, but the means by which God is accomplishing His great eternal purpose in His time.
> • Waiting patiently for God to make me more Christ like through people and circumstances when I want Him to give me a quick, preferably painless, fix.
> • Believing, in the midst of suffering and need, that God will be enough, that He will enable me to make it through.[21]

Do you believe that? Are you a *believing* believer?

Consider the mega-narrative of God's great plans. Haven't we totally underestimated our sin and its consequences? And haven't we totally underestimated God's love and grace? Then, can't we accept by faith that God will sometimes sacrifice temporal things for eternal things? Jesus asked, "What would you give in exchange for your soul?" (Mark 8:37)

Could God allow us to experience: abuse, disease, rape, divorce, childlessness, loss of a child, becoming a quadriplegic, loss of health, wealth, or career? Could God allow us: to have a disabled child we must care for our whole life, be rejected or misunderstood, lose our spouse, have a spouse with Alzheimer's, suffer with depression or whatever else could possibly happen to a human being? Could God allow any or all of these to happen for the greater good of growing our faith in Him, knowing that *faith* here is what connects me to God? Faith *is* my relationship to Him.

If you could choose, would you be willing to forfeit a pain-free life in order to gain your soul and live life to the fullest for all eternity—being right with God and enjoying Him forever? Would you? God can stop any of these "bad" things from happening. Why, sometimes, doesn't He? Could it be He has a greater good in mind for you? Would you trust Him to work it out? Do you believe "that God works all things together for good to those who love him"? (Romans 8:28) If you believed Him, how would this change your perspective about your trial?

Allow me to return to my original concern at the beginning of this chapter. Remember, Joseph had his dreams to help him endure his trials. However, what about the majority of us who didn't have a dream at the front end of our chronic trial? We don't always have the big dream revealing God's plan laid out ahead of time. But we do have the assurance of the Lord's presence with us now and the dream of being with the Most High God soon and forever. Anything and everything else pales to that. Do you believe that?

Helen Keller wrote, "Although the world is full of suffering, it is full also of the overcoming of it."[22]

"And this is the victory that has overcome the world—our faith." (1 John 5:4)

Chapter 8.
The Health of Holiness

Try to imagine a world without sin. There would be no lies, robberies, jails, locks, hospitals, wars, divorce, broken homes, boredom, loneliness, sorrow, regret, guilt, fear, lust, addictions, loss and most of the T.V. shows. It is because we are so saturated in this world by sin that it is hard to imagine heaven. Yet, heaven is not only the absence of sin, but the presence of holiness.

I would like to suggest that holiness is the health of the universe. Of all God's attributes, holiness seems to over-encompass all others. Because He is holy, He is good, loving and just. When Moses, Isaiah, Ezekiel and John saw a vision of God's presence and throne room, they were first affected by His holiness. They all had a deep sense of their own sin and His spiritual health. God is separate from sinners. Our God is "holy, innocent, unstained, separate from sinners and exalted above the heavens." (Hebrews 7:26) Hannah prayed, "There is no one holy like the Lord." (1 Samuel 2:2) John wrote, "God is light and in Him is no darkness at all." (1 John 1:5) The fact that God is holy is vital to the spiritual health of the universe.

Literally, holiness means to "cut a separation." There is a separation from all that is sinful and evil. We could say God is the absolute perfection of moral excellence, infinitely perfect in righteousness, purity and incomprehensible goodness. God is immaculate. God is the quintessence of spiritual health.

We see the holiness of God in the God-man, Jesus. He lived in a very sinful, dirty world, but was Himself without sin. He was in perfect harmony with His Holy Father. The Scriptures speak of the "beauty" of holiness. In the face of Jesus there is a glow, a glory, a radiance of holiness. At the cross, when He who knew no sin, became sin for us, we read that His face was marred beyond recognition. Jesus took on Himself our sin, and at that moment Jesus cried, "My God, My God, why have You forsaken Me?" Why? Because a holy separation was being made. The holy demands of God were met as the sinless One carried our sin to judgment.

Jesus said that those who were not whole needed a physician. God is the great physician, and yet, He is exceedingly more than that.

A. W. Tozer explained:

Holy is the way God is. To be holy He does not conform to a standard. He is that standard. He is absolutely holy with an infinite, incomprehensible fullness of purity that is incapable of being other than it is. Because He is holy, all His attributes are holy; that is, whatever we think of as belonging to God must be thought of as holy. God is holy and He has made holiness the moral condition necessary to the health of His universe. Sin's temporary presence in the world only accents this. Whatever is contrary to this is necessarily under His eternal displeasure. To preserve His creation God must destroy whatever would destroy it. When he arises to put down iniquity and save the world from irreparable moral collapse, He is said to be angry. Every wrathful judgment in the history of the world has been a holy act of preservation. The holiness of God, the wrath of God, and the health of creation are inseparably united. God's wrath is His utter intolerance of whatever degrades and destroys. He hates iniquity as a mother hates the polio that would take the life of her child.[23]

I encourage you to reread that quote and think about it. Also, please stick with me here as I connect these thoughts with our chronic pain.

Though your particular pain may not have resulted from your own sin, pain is ultimately a consequence of sin in this world. Pain may arise from the curse of sin in nature through natural disasters. Pain may come from someone else's sin causing you suffering. Or pain may stem from your own sin.

But we need to understand that though God is angry with sinners every day, if we are believers in Jesus Christ His anger has been spent on His Son through the cross on our behalf. So now, when He deals with us as believers, He does so through a loving discipline for the purpose of holiness. We will look at that very helpful consideration in a moment.

First, however, consider the work of a physician. He thumps you, cuts you, prescribes foul-tasting medicine, interferes with your normal pace of life, causes pain and suffering through tests, and often the treatment is quite disagreeable. He does not tell you what you want to hear. You may wish you could do without the process, but your health depends on his work and your cooperation. Some people may even appear healthy on the outside, but inside are riddled with deadly cancer.

I hear people say, "Sin is not that big of a deal." But, what if, from God's viewpoint, the greatness of sin is determined by the greatness of the One against whom it is committed? Then the guilt of sin is infinite, because it is a violation of the character of an infinitely Holy Being. "But your iniquities have made a separation between you and your God, and your sins have hidden His face from you so that He does not hear." (Isaiah 59:2) The psalmist noted, "There is no health in my bones because of my sin." (Psalm 38:3)

The diagnosis of evil present is shocking and disturbing—it is a matter of life and death—we need a drastic operation. We could choose to ignore it and live in temporary delusion; however, the disease is no respecter of persons.

God must remove our sin and impart to us His holiness, His spiritual health, His cure, which is nothing less than Himself. He does this by faith in the substitutionary death and resurrection of His Son Jesus. Jesus is the only remedy. "He Himself bore (carried) our sins in His body on the tree, that we might die to sin and live to righteousness. By His wounds you have been healed." (1 Peter 2:24)

Thirty years ago I had surgery for a rare bone disease. It was one of those good news/bad news situations. The good news was that the surgery was a success. The bad news was I got hepatitis from the anesthesia. There was nothing they could do, so I was sent home to either survive or die. One night, the family was called in to say good bye. God had other ideas, and from then on I began to get better. Fast forward 26 years. I went to the Mayo Clinic for a thorough check up. We discussed what happened with my liver. The doctor said, if that had happened today, they would have immediately done a liver transplant. He said, "In those days they sent you home to see if you would die or not." What we all need today for our sin problem is a life transplant. We need a new life.

That which His holiness demanded, His grace has provided through Jesus. We give Him our sin and He gives us His life—what an exchange! Contrary to what our culture is saying, there is only one remedy, only one cure, and that is Jesus.[24] God designed it that way. Do you believe His diagnosis? Have you received His cure? Someone aptly observed, "There is no sin so great that God will not forgive, but there is no sin so small that it does not need to be forgiven."

Before we discuss the discipline of the Lord in our lives as believers, I want to bring up something that is not often discussed—the subject of health at any cost. There are two issues here:

1. The first issue is the cost of holiness that we've been talking about. God will often sacrifice temporary things for eternal things. He may allow pain and suffering at many human levels to produce in us His holiness. In that sense there is no cost too high to be holy as He is holy. That is one reason we have been given the Holy Spirit to transform our character into the life and image of Christ.

2. The second issue is thinking that I must have my health back *at any cost!* We must keep things straight here. Holiness is essential for us, but our health is not. Don't get me wrong—we must be balanced. See a doctor; go to a counselor; use medications or natural remedies. It's okay to pursue health. Seeking our own health is part of the will to live both for quantity of years and for quality of life.

There is no inherent virtue in being sick. However, there is a balance even in that. Let me illustrate. A few years after coming down with a pain syndrome, I purchased a book about blood types for your health. I was desperate for solutions and this sounded reasonable since "the life is in the blood." I brought it home and without reading it went to bed. In the night I woke up with vivid demonic dreams. I didn't make the connection that night but prayed and read Scripture to get through the spiritual warfare. The next night the same thing happened. Though this was unusual for me I still didn't connect the dots. When it happened the third night I got up. The Lord had my full attention. I asked the Lord what was going on. Immediately my mind went to this book. I went and got it and discovered that this remedy was part of a far eastern religious cult. I threw it out in the garbage and never had the dream recur.

My point is this: Many remedies today are bringing along with them not holiness, or spiritual health, but rather further spiritual destruction, false religious ideas, eastern religions, and so forth. This reminds me of Jesus' words in Matthew 12:43-45. He told the story of a man who had an evil spirit come out of him. But then later the evil spirit came back and found his life unoccupied, so the evil spirit brought seven more even worse than himself and came and re-occupied the man. So this man's final condition was worse that at first. I've seen this happen. People get desperate and will do anything for health. Yet, some remedies bring certain spiritual destruction even worse than the illness itself.

Jesus asked, "What shall a man give in exchange for his soul?" (Mark 8:37) What will we exchange for our health? With what we've learned so far, if we have to choose one or the other, which is most important, my health or my holiness? Yes, sometimes it is not either/or, but when it is one or the other, which shall we choose?

Let me suggest, as a brother in Christ, ask the Lord for discernment when it comes to remedies. Pray for wisdom. Settle in your heart to what extent you will go to embrace a remedy. As a believer, the Holy Spirit resides in you. He will guide you into all truth. Holiness at any cost? Yes! Health at any cost? No! Count the cost. If a remedy interferes with our relationship with God, it is not of the Holy Spirit. Trust the promptings of the Holy Spirit. Trust the Scriptures. Trust God to carry you through the pain if there is no remedy for now. Let Him be your remedy. In fact, in our culture, health has become an idol—a god. Instead, let God be the God in your life.

Remember Isaiah's words, "In all their afflictions He was afflicted and the angel of His presence saved them; in His love and in His pity He redeemed them; He lifted them up and carried them all the days of old." (Isaiah 63:9) Jesus knows and feels your pain. And just like He carried your sin on the cross, He will carry you and me all our days. Augustine said, "Entrust the past to God's mercy, the present to His love, and the future to His providence."

Finally, I come to God's work of holiness in a believer's life through means of discipline. An older runner once said when asked about his commitment to running in his old age, "The pain of regret is greater than the pain of discipline." In other words, he would rather experience the pain involved in running, which was hard but what he loved, than wishing he had run and later having to live with the pain of regret.

As you embark on the last part of this chapter, please read Hebrews 12:1-17. I mentioned earlier that, when God deals with us as believers, He does so through a loving discipline for the purpose of spiritual health—holiness. Sin's penalty has been removed in Christ and sin's present power is broken. Through

Christ we can choose not to sin. Yet being still in these bodies, we are affected by sin's presence, fleshly patterns of sin and selfishness. That is why we are admonished to look at those who have gone before and lived in victory over sin. We are to "lay aside every weight and the sin which clings so closely." We all have particular besetting sins: pride, unbelief, bitterness, immorality and temporal mindedness. These would hinder our life race to the finish line. Run with endurance and look to Jesus. He initiates our faith and He carries us to the finish line, all by grace. When we are tempted to give up, we are to remember Jesus and all He went through. He died for us. We have not yet died; we're still living. So, with every breath, keep persevering.

God reminds us that sometimes our suffering is His discipline. Here are some truths to help us in this section:

1. God is addressing us as His children. We belong to Him. He is our Father. Discipline is evidence that we belong to God.

2. Don't take His discipline lightly. Be attentive. Take it seriously.

3. The motive behind all of His discipline is His love for us. He disciplines us because He loves us. His discipline is for our good, our benefit, just as we might expect from a good earthly father. God's motivation in our discipline is His perfect, divine love. He wouldn't discipline us if He didn't care. Isn't it funny how we turn things around? Chronic pain happens and we think God doesn't care. But God is saying here, "Because I care I am disciplining you."

4.   The purpose for all discipline is holiness, or spiritual health—unhindered relationship to God Himself. Is our relationship with Him not worth the suffering? He wants to share His healthy life with us to the fullest. This is why we were created. Though trials often bring questions and mystery, there is no mystery in God's purpose for discipline—our holiness.

5.   With discipline there is a time element involved. At present, discipline feels unpleasant and painful. "But later" discipline yields the fruit of a healthy relationship to God—if we allow His discipline to train us. You see, chronic pain and suffering doesn't guarantee good fruit. Only when we allow His holiness in, does His discipline transform us. Are we believing by faith that God is working His holiness in us, and are we cooperating with Him in it?

6.   Also, we sometimes assume that God disciplines us *only* as punishment for our sin. One of the most common phrases among sufferers is, "What did I do to deserve this!?" But remember, God's discipline is much broader than punishment. He often disciplines us in the sense that a father trains his child for righteous living (see Hebrews 12:7-11).

You see, discipline by God for the believer is a part of redemptive suffering. Because our heavenly Father loves us more than we can fully comprehend, He will purposely allow discipline in our lives motivated by this unconditional, extravagant, perfect and unending love for the purpose of working in us His holiness. This work in us is very personal to God. I find it is easier to suffer with a purpose. I believe what we see in Scripture is that all suffering is *full of purpose* for us as believers.

We may never uncover a humanly rational purpose for our suffering in our lifetime. But we can always be assured of God's overarching purpose in our suffering—to present us holy before Him. Because without holiness, no one will see God—a condition that would be the greatest suffering imaginable.

The last few verses from Hebrews 12:1-17 get even more personal. Have you ever felt like giving up? Who else could you turn to? Maybe you don't want to give up on God, but would like to give up this life of suffering. I have literally asked God hundreds of times to take me home. I was so tired and exhausted. I just didn't want to go on. This happened one particular day at death's door. God turned my thinking around with a Psalm. It is amazing how the truth can set us free in our thinking. In a very dark hour, I thought—what is the greatest gift—LIFE. Yet my life was miserable with pain. Then God reminded me of Psalm 63:3 (NKJV), "Because Your loving kindness is *better than life*, my lips shall praise you." What is even better than life itself? To know *God* loves us. He *loves* us. He loves *us*. The simplest yet most profound truth in all the universe is that God loves us. His love is not based on our performance or lack thereof, but simply stems from His choice to love us. When will we ever get it? God loves us. Jesus proved it forever. Do we believe Him?

My hands, my knees and my heart were drooping that day. I was spiritually dry, broken and lame. Some of my thoughts were lame, but God spoke encouragement to me. He gave me peace, even enough to share with others.

In another chapter we will look at grace deeper. But here, suffice it to say, all we need we have from God and it all comes by grace. Among other things, grace is God's ability and provision for us so that we will not give up. As a genuine believer we will not ultimately fail. Praise the LORD! At times we may fail to lay hold of His grace and be totally miserable. But at that point we're admonished, "see to it that no one fails to obtain the grace of God." The writer of Hebrews then mentions three root sins all stemming from the pride of unbelief: 1) A root of bitterness; 2) Sexual immorality in all its forms; and 3) Temporal-mindedness (see Hebrews 12:15-29).

All three of these root sins were evident in the life of Esau. These sins may keep unbelievers from turning to God, and these sins can dog us as believers, clinging to us as "weights".

What is the antidote for all sin? The divine grace gift of repentance. For Esau the pain of regret was far greater than any of his trials because he never repented. He never truly turned in faith to God.

I like what Warren Wiersbe says:

> We must correctly distinguish regret, remorse and repentance. *Regret*: is an activity of the mind; whenever we remember what we've done, we ask ourselves, "Why did I do that?" *Remorse* includes both the heart and the mind and we feel disgust and pain but we don't change our ways. *True Repentance* includes the mind, the heart and the will. We change our mind about our sins, and agree with what God says about them; we abhor ourselves because of what we've done; and we deliberately turn from our sin and turn to the Lord for His mercy. [25]

So, are you being disciplined in your trial? Don't beat yourself up. Jesus was already beat up for you. By God's grace, accept His love, embracing the grace of repentance and be patient, giving God time to finish the great work of faith, which is the overcoming victory and holiness without which none of us will see God. That is a healthy response.

Chapter 9.
The Grace Place

As I write this chapter, millions of foreclosures are taking place across our nation. Many families are being displaced, often with nowhere to go. To be homeless is a very frightening situation especially if you have loved ones for whom you're responsible. We often read of the refugees fleeing their homeland, running to another country where they are not welcome. They are homeless and country-less. This is always a sad, desperate situation. Yet, there is a worse place to be—graceless, left in sin.

A living, eternal soul needs a place, a place to call home—a place of rest and refuge. We all need a *grace place*. In Romans 5:2, Paul tells us that a relationship with Jesus provides us with a place to stand and a reason to rejoice. At the point of entrance to this grace place we find repentance and faith. Jesus took our place on the cross and died for our sins. The repentance of faith gives us entrance into a relationship with Jesus—the grace place.

Before we relate all this to chronic suffering though, I want us to see a pattern in the Bible. I want us to see the great importance of *place*. There were preliminary grace places and also places where grace had been rejected.

In the beginning God created space, matter and time. Here we'll focus on space or particular places. God gave a place to the firmament and the earth; to darkness and light; a place for water and a place for land. He geographically arranged individuals and nations. Certain places were designated by God for special purposes—places were separated out. God prepared a place called Eden for Adam and Eve. This was a grace place of provision and God's favor.

God called Abraham to a special place called Mt. Moriah where He tested him by requiring him to sacrifice his son, Isaac. When Abraham followed through to the point of obedience, God stepped in and provided His own sacrifice, a ram. So Abraham called the place Jehovah Jireh, or "The Lord will provide."

Later, when Jacob dreamed of a ladder to heaven, he proclaimed, "Surely the Lord is in this place." God confirmed His covenant with Jacob. Jacob named the place where God spoke to Him, Bethel, "the gate of heaven."

Joseph was enslaved in a place of confinement for many years. It was a place of chronic suffering until God was ready to use him for special purposes. Joseph had to learn his place. He said to his brothers, "Do not fear, for am I in the place of God? As for you; you meant evil against me, but God meant it for good, to bring about that many people should be kept alive, as they are today." (Genesis 50:19) Joseph's question serves as a good question for us in our suffering: "Am I in the [position] of God?" God knows what He is doing. We must grant Him His rightful place as God.

Moses met God at a place called the burning bush. He was called to lead the children of Israel out of Egypt—the place of slavery and bondage. In the law, Moses was to set up certain places for the innocent to run to, called cities of refuge. These were safe zones until thorough investigation acquitted them.

Joshua led the people of Israel into the Promised Land. This was an Old Testament grace place for Israel—a place of blessing, rest, abundance and security. The Promised Land was given by God and entered by faith. Every place the sole of their foot touched was theirs.

First in the tabernacle and later in the more permanent temple were special places to worship God and sacrifice for sin. Separating the holy place from the Most Holy Place was a veil—a thick curtain. Only once a year on the Day of Atonement was the high priest allowed to enter with a blood sacrifice to meet God. Eventually evil places, called high places, were set up all over Israel which spread the false worship of idolatry. The wrong places of worship included wrong approaches to right worship, which cost many people their lives. There was one proper place to worship God—the Most Holy Place.

Job brought up a good point when he asked, "And where is the place of understanding?" (Job 28:12, 20) Then he answers his own question, "God understands the way to it and He knows its place." (Job 28:23) Then God turns to mankind and says, "Behold, the fear of the Lord, that is wisdom, and to turn away from evil is understanding."(Job 28:28) God has revealed the place of understanding to us—a right relationship with Him!

The psalmists speak of darkness as God's secret place. Maybe the darkness we sometimes find ourselves in—in which we assume God is not present—is actually the shadow of the Almighty! (Psalm 91:1) The psalmists speak of God being our *hiding place, strong tower* and *place of refuge*. I love when it says, "He brought me out into a broad *place*; He rescued me, because He delighted in me." (Psalm 18:19) In the grace place, we know that God delights in us in a big way.

The great prophet Isaiah reminds us, "For thus says the One who is high and lifted up, who inhabits eternity, whose name is Holy: 'I dwell in the high and holy *place*, and also with him who is of a contrite and lowly spirit, to revive the spirit of the lowly and to revive the heart of the contrite.'" (Isaiah 57:15) God is above space, matter and time as Creator and invites us to Himself through humility and contrition.

Both Daniel and Matthew speak of the Abomination of Desolation standing in the holy *place*. This occurs during the midpoint of the seven years of tribulation when the Antichrist enters the holy *place* of the Jewish temple. He desecrates it because he is unauthorized and unclean. One of Daniel's visions for the end-times shows the nations pulverized with no *place* left for them. Imagine a country-less country.

Then we come to Jesus full of grace and truth. He was born in a manger because there was no *place* for Him in the inn. Foxes had holes; birds had nests; but the Son of man had no *place* to call home after age 30. Yet Jesus would often retreat to a solitary *place*. He told unbelievers, "My word has no *place* in you." (John 8:37) He told His followers, "I go to prepare a *place* for you." (John 14:2) Some found no *place* for repentance. We are exhorted not to give *place* to the Devil. Jesus was crucified at Golgotha—the *place* of a skull.

We learn from Scripture that a spirit needs a body, a *place* to call home. When the spirit leaves the body the body is dead. Even unclean spirits seem to need a body. (Matthew 12:43-45) Jesus gave up His spirit to the Father, and then His body died.

We learn that God determines the times and *places* people live. (Acts 17:26) He strategically does this to allow people to seek Him and find Him—sheer grace. We are told as believers our bodies are the dwelling *place* of the Holy Spirit. We can worship Him in spirit and in truth, rather than being limited to a geographic worship *place*. (I Corinthians 6:19-20)

I said all that to say this: the only authorized and authentic *place* of meeting and enjoying God is the *place* of a person—Jesus Christ. Jesus Christ is the *Grace Place*.

The story is told of the prairie farmer in the early days of America who saw a wind-swept prairie fire racing toward his home and family. To save his family, he lit a controlled fire around his home which burned off an area that he and his family could then stand in. When the large, destructive fire arrived, it went around the already burned area and saved their lives. The analogy is obvious—Jesus is the controlled burn of judgment. God poured out His wrath against our sin on Jesus. He saves us from the coming wrath of God on Judgment Day. If we now stand by faith in Christ, we will be saved. He is the *Grace Place*, safe from God's wrath. "There is now no condemnation to those who are *in Christ*." (Romans 8:1)

Yet, our position of relationship in Jesus Christ is so much more than merely escape from judgment. Our relationship with Christ is *abundant life*. The *Grace Place* is a position of relationship in Christ, a place of right standing with and blessing from God right now. We enter by believing in Jesus—all that He is for all that I need (especially as sin-bearer). Once we enter the *Grace Place* we are justified—declared righteous by God. Our right-standing with God brings peace, something every sufferer desperately needs. And our right-standing with God brings depth of soul, satisfaction and rest.

Through Jesus, the door to the *Grace Place*, we enter into a realm of genuine life in Christ. In us and we in Him, Jesus becomes our very life. This is a new *place* for us. This is a *place* to stand with God—loved, delighted in, and fully accepted. This is the *place* of understanding our condition. We are now in the *place* of God's favor—"in Christ".

We must understand that grace is not merely a cold theological term. Grace is not stagnant, irrelevant or untested. True grace is living, relevant and proven. God's grace moves us in a growth process of relationship that is very dynamic and life altering. We recognize the relevance of and our desperate need for God's grace when we're tested. God's grace, in which we stand by faith, produces *endurance* during trials, resulting in *strength of character*. And as God *strengthens our character*, He produces *hope* in us. Hope is the quality God provides to sustain us through trials to the *better end*. (See Romans 5:1-5.)

Sometimes in our suffering, when we break through the dark clouds of despair into the glorious light of our position in Christ, we experience so much joy and peace that we think, "Surely God will now take away all my suffering." It's true, sometimes God merely uses our suffering to bring us to this place of dependence in Him and then He heals us. And our realization of the great grace of God is so wonderful, we expect it to usher in healing. But in spite of this glorious realization of our Grace Place in Him, He may yet have other things planned for us and choose not to heal us.

The fact that we are not healed does not render our realization of our stance in Jesus any less glorious or wonderful. In fact, because of our realization we now have new hope and purpose in enduring our sufferings. When your trial exceeds the time limits of your brokenness and strength, and whatever else brought you to that place, from there on, it's building character in you for the glory of God. The Grace Place is the place of deep abiding soul rest. This truth is an anchor of hope knowing all is well between God and you and also better days are ahead either in the land of the living or in heaven itself.

So character building in trials builds anchoring hope. This is very important, so stay with me! Hope and character re-move the shame of suffering because God's love, through the Holy Spirit is poured into our hearts. A hope without character leaves us in a place of self-condemnation. Both character and hope are needed. Never despise God's character building or think that it's not that important. This character building is vital because it's the very transforming life of Jesus encouraging us in the hope (assurance) of being like Him someday. This trans-formation is God's design for us. And all through this process we are bathed in the river of God's love which is personally and intimately ministered to us by His Holy Spirit. These are God's ways. We must learn them. Don't be ashamed of the humilia-tion of your trial. God gives more grace to the humble.

The Grace Place is the place in my heart that I run to daily where God not only loves me, but *likes* me. He is not in a per-petual state of being "ticked off" with me. He's not a reluctant Savior. Because of sin's presence in our lives we seem to think, "God loves me because the Bible tells me so, but surely He doesn't *like* me. Sometimes I'm not sure I like me!"

The Grace Place is the place of knowing that God ac-cepts us not because of what we do or don't do, but because of what Jesus did and does on our behalf. God accepts us be-cause of who we are in Christ, not what we do. I've often said true Christianity is a performance based life—it's just not *our* performance—but JESUS'! Of Jesus the Father said, "This is my beloved Son in whom I am well pleased." (Matthew 3:17) And Jesus reminded us that we are infinitely more valuable than a bird or a flower, even though God lovingly cares for them too. So, unpack, rest, delight and revel in God's grace. It's the place you can finally be yourself—who God created you to be. Paul said, "I am what I am by the grace of God." (1 Corinthians 5:10) It is the "not-I-but-Christ-life." Grace is Christ living His life through us individually. It is the place where we recognize that God is infinitely bigger than our sin, our circumstances, our failures, our successes, and our mind-limiting questions.

The Grace Place is the place of the *Great Exchange*. I give Jesus my sin and He gives me His life. No sin is too big for grace and no sin is too small not to need grace. The Grace Place is not living in the law of condemnation, but in the new law of the Spirit of life in Christ. The Grace Place is a place of being very uncomfortable with sin even after the initial pleasure, because sin is now unnatural to who I am in Christ. As a transformed follower of Christ, I do not want to live in sin; I am dead to it and now I live to God. The Grace Place is where Jesus is not simply *part* of my life, He is my very life. The Grace Place is a profound life changing union. Jesus said: "My yoke is easy and my burden is light." (Matthew 11:30) You are fully accepted in Christ. Do you believe this?

Grace is Jesus—a deep abiding, growing, living, relationship with Jesus—a place where God's strength is found to be sufficient in my weakness. Grace is God's life poured out to sinners. God had to stoop to do this. Grace is like a three-fold cord of the Godhead wrapping up all His attributes into one and lassoing us from the sea of destruction. The grace of God is as vast as God Himself. Grace is the unmerited love and favor of God toward an undeserving sinner. Grace is not only acquittal from the Judge, but *The Judge* jumping over the bench, offering to pay your penalty and then giving you His own wealth. It's just amazing isn't it? God is for you, loves you, likes you and delights in you! Do you believe this? It will change you inside-out no matter what your circumstances are.

You see, God delights in choosing the most unworthy and undesirable and making them the objects of His love and acceptance (2 Corinthians 8:9). God in Christ has laid the mantle of His favor on you. What gives you and me significance is receiving His grace. Grace changes everything! But it takes time and often is messy. I needed to learn that. It's not always neat, tidy and box-like. Grace prevails through messy relationships, trials and circumstances often not of our choosing. God is at work, not so much mechanically—immediately changing our circumstances, but more biologically—transforming us from the inside out. Let Him change you. Joseph had God's favor all over him, yet God left him in prison longer than he wanted.

Have you been humbled by your trial? Is your life a mess emotionally, financially, mentally, physically, even spiritually? Has God said, "No" to your big prayer of deliverance *from* your trial? Could it be that God is gracing you to deliver you *through* your trial? Look for the myriad of little graces everyday. Be alert to them. Give God thanks for them. Maybe the answers to your questions are staring you in the face. Let's allow Jesus to come between us and our circumstances.

Accordingly, grace has some things to teach us along the way (Titus 2:11-14). Grace is freeing to us, not with the freedom to sin, but the freedom to glorify God. Grace teaches us character, things like—denying ungodliness and worldly lusts and to live soberly, righteously and godly in this present age. It is "the law of the Spirit of life in Christ" which sets us free from sin's habitual grasp. Why is this important to our discussion on suffering? Because, in our suffering, we are tempted to compensate for our pain with temporal and fleshly counterfeit pleasures.

That's one reason why people sometimes binge shop after a disappointing week. "We owe it to ourselves after all we've been through." Others may binge on lust, alcohol, drugs, or self-pity. The psalmist reminds us though, "You make known to me the path of life; in Your presence there is fullness of joy; at Your right hand are pleasures forevermore." (Psalm 16:11) Sin and counterfeit compensation take us down a path of death. Jesus graciously takes us up the path of life to full joy and forever pleasures—not quick, fleeting fixes.

Do you believe this? In the depth of your chronic pain, will you believe Jesus? Will you believe God for His provision of grace that Jesus is all you need? Charles Spurgeon reminds us, "He restored more than was ever taken away from us....grace has so much more abounded that, *in Jesus* we have *regained* more than in Adam we lost. Our paradise regained is far more glorious than our paradise lost."[26] God will restore more than the locusts have eaten. Because of grace, Jesus does not pay us as our sins deserve. I pray this gives your inner being hope.

Let Jesus increase. Let go to God, and let yourself be decreased. For it is in losing that we gain. Unpack your bags here in the Grace Place. If you have genuinely confessed your sin, now believe God. Stand with Jesus. Let God's Spirit reduce, confine, crowd, undo, unravel, break and put you in His place, the Grace Place.

In the prison of pain, Joseph learned to live in the Grace Place. His soul entered the iron, the furnace of affliction, but it came out refined and glorious to God. You are never alone. You stand seated in the heavenly *places* with Jesus in the grace place. You will triumph—grace will see to it. Yes, there is a cross and a burial place, but the disciples simply *saw* the place where He *had lain*; but He was not there. He was risen, just as He said.

Now in grace, so are you. You are raised with Christ—rejoice and be glad in your standing. I agree with Pastor Chuck Swindol, We need a "grace awakening." Let it start with me.

In Your Presence[27]

The fresh dew of morning, the first light of day,
In the dawn—a new beginning, my heart is swept away
To the Throne Room of Your heart, O Lord, my home, my hiding place
To dine with You, and gaze upon—the beauty of Your face.

Lord Jesus, in Your Presence—there is nothing else I need,
Just to know You in the stillness, in quietness and peace.
Your love is irresistible; Your arms are open wide
As you lovingly and joyfully welcome me inside.

To the Throne Room of Your Heart, O Lord, my home my hiding place;
I enter Your sweet Presence—and feast upon Your grace.
The morning dew of heaven in the dawn of this new day,
The glory of my Savior's love will strengthen, comfort, stay—
Until the day we see His face and bow before His Throne.
We live; we love; we worship Him—for He is Christ the Lord!

Chapter 10.
Time Trials— (How Long?)

David asked the question every chronic sufferer at some point asks: "How long, O Lord? Will you forget me forever? How long will you hide your face from me? How long must I wrestle with my thoughts and everyday have sorrow in my heart? How long will my enemy triumph over me?" (Psalm 13:1-2 NIV)

As a believer, deep down you know God is listening and observing. You know from His Word He will never leave you nor forsake you. You have cried out to God. You have confessed your sin. You have worked harder, gritting your teeth. You may have made "deals" with God, "If you heal me I'll serve you." Yet, there is only silence. Days turn to weeks, which turn to months, and now it's been years. Suffering has become a large segment of your lifetime. Your soul has entered the iron of affliction. There is no end in sight. Nothing ever changes except maybe you are wearing down.

In the beginning, God created time—the evening and the morning were the first day. After six days of creation, God concluded the week with a day of rest. The clock was ticking. God said all his created works were "good." As Creator, God is not bound by time. When it comes to His creation, He sovereignly rules over it to accomplish His purposes. Time is a gift to mankind. Time measures experience. Time gives us a history—

things to look back on and remember. Time gives us a story, a meta-narrative of God's over all plan, but time also records our personal story.

Time also provides us with a future—things to look forward to. But mostly, time embraces the present moment. We are each given an allotment of time called a life-time. Time allows us to mark experience and it gives us present opportunity. The key opportunity God gives each of us is to believe Him. We will see shortly that time is vital for faith to be real and exercised.

The Bible reveals to us that God is eternal. I won't pretend to understand that. God inhabits eternity, but works in time. God *is* eternal life. For our understanding, this means that quantitatively God has no beginning and no end. From everlasting to everlasting He is God. On the timeline of human experience, God was infinitely present in both directions—past and future. Yet, even that last statement is not totally accurate because of the word "was". God the Father and God the Son both revealed themselves as the great "I AM". The eternally existing One, Jesus, as Creator of the universe existed before time. Yet, at just the "right time", in the "fullness of time," God sent Jesus to earth as a man to die for our sins. (Galatians 4:4)

An inadequate, yet helpful, example for us might be to picture time as a line in two dimensions with a starting point and an ending point. The quality of eternal life is more dimensional—it encompasses both the timeline and three dimensional space in every direction around it. In other words, eternity is not just an extension of time—it completely transcends it as much and more, as a life transcends a pencil line on a piece of paper. Eternity is linked inseparably to God's life—it can't be measured. All explanations are utterly inadequate, yet a biblical study of eternity reveals not simply quantity of time, but so much more—the quality of God's abiding presence. Jesus said He came to bring life more abundantly. He says, "And this is eternal life, that they may know you, the only true God, and Jesus Christ whom you have sent." (John 17:3) So, eternal life is knowing God intimately and personally.

I have often thought of eternity expressed as the *present* tense. Maybe that's why for the believer everything past and future is a present reality (in Christ). By faith, I can now enter into His death, burial and resurrection (past in time, yet present). Yet, I'm already seated with Christ in the heavenly places (future in time, yet present). And perhaps our loved ones, who have died years ago, will think no time has elapsed when they see us again. These are all amazing thoughts because our God is eternal!

In Ecclesiastes Solomon wrote of God, "He has made everything beautiful in its time. Also, He has put eternity in their hearts, except that no one can find out the work that God does from beginning to end." (Ecclesiastes 3:11 NKJV) Every person has the concept of eternity in their heart; because God put it there. Our difficulty with this is that we are so limited. We are not God, so we aren't able to fully integrate time and eternity. What we do know is this, "I know whatever God does, it shall be forever. Nothing can be added to it, and nothing taken from it. God does it, that men should fear before Him." (Ecclesiastes 3:14 NKJV)

"Our compulsive timetables collide with God's leisurely providence".[28] Eternity outweighs time. God works at a different pace than we do. Someone said, "patience is allowing God time to work [in a difficult situation] without giving Him a deadline to remove it." You see, the great characteristic of heaven is the will of God and that His will shall be done. We pray "Your will be done on earth as it is in heaven." The great human need is to get in alignment and submission with God's will. Only a faith connection with Jesus can accomplish this.

One of my daughters recently had twins. I have observed that these two little ones sleep best lying on Mom and Dad's chests listening to their hearts beat. Jesus invites us to come to Him and rest from our labors and enter His rest, listening to His heart beat, or as Eugene Peterson renders it, "the unforced rhythms of grace." (Matthew 11:28-30 MSG) As we discover, God's will is actually easy and light; it's a good fit. God acts on behalf of the one who waits for Him.

So how long must we wait for deliverance from our suffering? As I said earlier, time is vital for faith to be real and exercised. If you have a trial and it ends before it starts, you don't need faith. Faith to operate needs a duration of time, a time span for the purpose of trust and growth. "To everything there is a season, a time for every purpose under heaven." (Ecclesiastes 3:1 NKJV) The longer the trial, the deeper the faith.

Remember, Joseph had been in prison for about 13 years. Two men, Pharaoh's baker and butler also landed in prison. Both had dreams about their fate. Joseph interpreted the dreams and connected them to reality. On Pharaoh's birthday the baker was hanged and the butler was restored to his position with the king. Joseph asked the butler to mention his case to the king. Maybe this would be his freedom; but the butler forgot about Joseph for two full years. Finally, when the king had a dream and wanted it interpreted, the butler remembered Joseph and mentioned him to Pharaoh. Note, however, that the butler didn't mention Joseph's situation, just that he could interpret dreams. Joseph interpreted the dream and was exalted next in command to the king.

In this life, this side of eternity, timing is very important in trials of our faith. All of us can think of near death experiences where the timing made all the difference. Split second alterations and the results would've been totally different. What if Joseph had been remembered two years earlier and even released. The king may not have had his dream; Joseph would possibly have gone home, and two whole nations would have starved to death in the famine. The implications are enormous; the scenarios are many.

Without the wisdom of God and His gracious providence, we have no clue how precise and accurate God is in His timing. Like a Heavenly Baker baking bread, God not only uses the right ingredients in the proper amounts, but He turns the oven on at the right temperature and then bakes the bread for the length of time for best results. Faith trials of chronic pain are much like that. The ingredients by themselves, yet unbaked are distasteful and even repulsive. Then, God turns up the heat, the furnace of affliction. We think He's burning us. He's not. And when we think we should only be in the oven for 10 minutes and He leaves us in for an hour, we squirm. But, when we cooperate, out comes the most delicious home-made bread you have ever smelled or tasted.

The Bible says, "Taste and see that the Lord is good." (Psalm 34:8 NKJV) and "Now thanks be to God who always leads us in triumph in Christ, and through us diffuses the fragrance of His knowledge in every place". (2 Corinthians 2:14 NKJV)

By grace we are given perseverance and asked to exercise it. Perseverance is the quality of genuine faith that enables us to continue to the end. It is a very powerful grace. Jesus prayed that Peter's faith would not fail (Luke 22:31-32). Peter did persevere and later wrote out of his experience for our benefit, "Who are kept by the power of God, through faith, for salvation, ready to be revealed in the last time." (1 Peter 1:4 NKJV) Paul said, "He who has begun a good work in you will complete it." (Philippians 1:6) Jesus is the author and finisher of our faith. Do you believe this? Let us work out what God is working in. Paul said at the end of his life, "I have fought the good fight, I have finished the race, I have kept the faith." (2 Timothy 4:7 NKJV) The whole book of Hebrews admonishes believers to persevere.

Trust God for His perfect timing and duration. Mary and Martha had to learn this. Jesus could have healed their brother Lazarus before he died. But Jesus waited a few extra days, allowed him to die and then showed the world that He is the resurrection and the life by raising him from the dead. By the way, this event catapulted other events into the crucifixion week of Jesus. In the same way with us, God is writing a much bigger story and we are an important part of it. Just let God author it. Let patience have its perfect work. "In this you greatly rejoice, though now, *for a little while*, if need be, you have been grieved by various trials, that the genuineness of your faith—being much more precious than gold that perishes, though tested by fire—may be found to praise, honor, and glory at the revelation of Jesus Christ." (1 Peter 1:6-7 NKJV)

In chronic suffering there is a time element—a waiting period that tests and reveals our faith. Time both strengthens our faith and proves it genuine. Genuine faith takes us much further than we ever thought we could or would have wanted to go. Paul said he and his co-workers were "burdened beyond measure, above strength, so that we despaired even of life." (2 Corinthians 1:8) He said it was like a death sentence, and yet, he didn't die. God wanted to deliver Paul *through* the trial by having him trust God in it.

Have you ever wanted to die? Have you ever asked God to take you home? I have. It was my prayer every day for 12 years. God didn't answer those prayers as I thought He should. Thankfully, He knows what He is doing! My painful condition was like waking up every morning with the same noose around my neck. The iron collar was clamped around my neck. I could hardly breathe. I just wanted to die. Intensity of pain was part of it, but duration of time was also part of it. Down deep I never wanted to give up on God—I had no one else big enough to fill His shoes. I desperately needed Him and wanted Him, yet every fiber of my faith was being stretched. I began to see I couldn't give up on Him because He wasn't going to let go of me.

I verbalized my feelings to Him. Very fervently, but reverently, I pleaded for answers. He quietly said, "My grace is sufficient for you." I began to see like Job that answers aren't always adequate, *but God is.* He became my Answer! He let me peek into 1 Peter 5:10, "But may the God of all grace, who called us to His eternal glory by Christ Jesus, *after* you have *suffered a while*, perfect, establish, strengthen, and settle you. To Him be the glory and dominion forever and ever, Amen." Did you notice the word "after"? Did you notice how long—"a while"?

When you get a chance, read the story in Luke 16:19-31 of the rich man and Lazarus. Among the many things we can learn from this story, I note the following two things:

- Lifetimes between individuals can display great discrepancies. The rich man lived in luxury every day. The beggar couldn't walk or work, had to beg for crumbs every day, and had a chronic illness full of sores. He lived with the dogs. That was a reality snapshot of their lives—their lifetimes.

- Notice the eternal flip-flop: Abraham speaking to the rich man said: "Son, remember that in your *lifetime* you received your good things, and *likewise* Lazarus evil things; *but now*, he is comforted and you are tormented." (Luke 16:25) The lesson isn't so much about money—it is about faith. (Luke 16:29-31) Faith changes everything. It is precious to God.

Are you living a lifetime of chronic pain and suffering? Rejoice! See the joy set before you. For a long time I said I felt like I was standing still and the whole world was passing me by. I was missing out on life. I had lost valuable time to work and accomplish things. Then I thought of two people: 1) Lazarus—after death, life flip-flopped for him; and, 2) Joseph—in one day life flip-flopped for him—from 13 years of prison to the king's right-hand man. I actually began to feel honored that I was chosen to suffer. Don't get me wrong—I don't like it or want it, but I began to see God's wisdom and value in it.

Dear friend, if God has called you to suffer over time, there will come an end to it. Either by healing like Joseph or through death like Lazarus. Either way you win, because (faith + grace) x time = glory in eternity. Remember, life is short—it is like a dissipating vapor, a fleeting cloud or a fading flower, here today and gone tomorrow. Don't even focus so much on life spans—why God takes a child at 11 or another person at 95. The greatest person of faith I've ever known was an eleven year old friend who died of leukemia. Did he lose out on life—some would say yes, but because eternity entered his little life at an early age, he actually entered into fuller life—the life of God. His faith was way beyond his years.

Let Jesus author and finish your faith. Let Him build the character of His own life in and through you. Take advantage of this time. Allow Him to develop patience and perseverance. Develop godly tenacity, the stubborn persistence and unwillingness to acknowledge defeat, because your faith is the victory that overcomes the world.

Wait on God. Stay the course with expectation and readiness and hope. Rest in the Lord. Get up every day and do what you know to do. Get dressed, eat breakfast, change the diaper, get the mail, read your Bible, etc. Trust the Lord with all your heart and don't lean to your own understanding. "Wait on the Lord; be of good courage, and He shall strengthen your heart; wait I say on the Lord." (Psalm 27:14 NKJV) Be full of (good) courage—the kind of courage that trusts in God, not yourself. When it comes to Jesus—no one can pluck us out of His hand.

Be diligent. Be energetic with whatever strength you have. Be painstaking in your faith. Be steadfast, immovable, stay the course, be brave, carry on, overcome, get the better of your situation. Take the opportunity of time to draw close to God—maybe that is all the energy you have. Occupy yourself with worship. Be determined—make that definite decision to follow Jesus. If He leads you into a time of suffering, keep following. Fix your heart in Him. Ask for divine mettle, that strength of spirit, that Holy Spirit bravery we desperately need. And when the Lord returns, will He find faith on the earth? Yes, He will find it in you.

Remember, dear friends, there is a difference between God's appointed time and the times that we expect. Our expectations must be in God and Him alone, not in perceived timetables and schedules for removal. Misplaced expectations, clock watching or making deals with God to put a deadline on things can result in anger, bitterness and very often in chronic pain and depression. "My soul, wait silently for God alone. For my expectation is from Him." (Psalm 62:5 NKJV)

So, how long, O Lord? The answer: Until God says enough—no sooner, no later. Trust the Heavenly Baker. He's already given us the Bread of Life, Jesus. "If God be for us, who can be against us? He who did not spare His own Son, but delivered Him up for us all, how shall He not with Him also freely give us all things?" (Romans 8:32)

In the middle of chronic adversity we feel like we are standing still and the world is passing us by. Year after year and nothing significant seems to change; time seems wasted, but in reality we are being catapulted years ahead by the very things we think have slowed us down. Could it be that chronic suffering takes us to a different dimension both eternal and spiritual and then prepares and places us ahead of our time to comfort, provide, protect, persevere and become an example for others? Could it be that a famine is on the way, a time of loss and need for others and that God is preparing us and sending us ahead to save lives as He did with Joseph? Everything comes at the proper time to him who knows how to wait.

"The person who doesn't learn patience will have a difficult time learning anything else."[29]

Chapter 11.
Suffering on Purpose

One of the most difficult things in life is to suffer without a reason. If what you are suffering has no ultimate meaning or purpose, no divine reason, then maybe the journey just isn't worth it. I personally have known a number of people who either never knew the great purpose behind their suffering or just lost sight of it. Life just wasn't worth living. They took their own lives. While the Bible doesn't teach that suicide is the unpardonable sin, it is still a sin because it takes from God what is rightfully His—our life.

If you have suffered deeply for a long time, you know what I'm talking about. You may not have considered suicide, but you may have prayed everyday for years that God would just take you home. Your soul entered so deeply into your iron of suffering and pain that you just didn't want to live on. I understand that. I've experienced it. You agree with Paul that to be with Christ is far better than remaining here. However, like Paul, all believers in Christ must come to the ultimate submission of yielding not only our lives to Him, but also the timing of our death. I encourage you to read Joni Eareckson Tada's book on this whole subject called, *When Is It Right to Die?*

You see, chronic pain over time can affect our perception of life. "If you wallow in self-pity, then the pictures of pain will become mirrors, and all you will see is yourself."[30] Such a view is too small. It is not big enough to see us through. As we've seen, God uses suffering to grow our faith and character; to accomplish a bigger story involving others (like Joseph's story); and as a means for equipping us to help and comfort others on their journey. God provides a bigger, grander purpose for our trial that is greater than any level of human suffering.

If you are not a follower of Jesus Christ, there is no greater meaning to your suffering right now than to see it as a means of bringing you to a saving knowledge of Christ. In your present circumstances, that is God's grand design for your pain. If you are a follower of Jesus Christ, then every bit of pain and suffering has ultimate meaning and purpose.

Let me keep this real, and not sugar-coat the situation. What about the pain of the father who backed over and killed his two year old daughter? What about the 18 year old son brain-damaged from a vehicle rollover? What about the son who went camping at a popular lake and drowned, whose body was never found? What about the godly parents whose godly teenage daughter was brutally raped? What about the family whose grandpa and father committed suicide and now the son is making attempts at it? What about the spouse with Alzheimer's? How about the messy divorce? How do we reckon with the worship leader who committed suicide because his pain was so intense from an injury?

And we could go on with other types of human suffering. I think of the single woman in her 50's that always wanted to be married. Or how about the couple who could never have children? Consider the person who has been in prison for years for a crime they never committed. Is there something bigger than all this suffering that gives it meaning and purpose? Yes! Yes! Yes!

The human tragedies I've listed above are real, very real. But friends, there is a greater truth, a greater eternal, infinite reality that is seen through the eyes of faith that enters a much weightier realm. Our spiritual forefathers expressed the ultimate reason for which we were created, "The chief end of man is to glorify God and enjoy Him forever." John Piper has rightly exchanged *and* for *by* which connects our purpose with enjoyment. (That is, we glorify God *by* enjoying Him forever!) So let's apply our God-given purpose to our suffering:

"The chief end [purpose] of my pain is to glorify God by enjoying Him forever."

The only thing big enough to see us through our pain *and* to actually attach longer-than-life and bigger-than-life meaning to it is God Himself. God is greater than all my problems. The glory of God is the ultimate purpose of the universe and the only thing worthy of human suffering.

Mark Twain said, "It's not what we don't know about God that should upset us, but what we do know." Let's turn that around: because of what we do know about God, what we don't know about Him should encourage and comfort us. We think that the book of Job is primarily about suffering, but the main topic and character is God Himself. In the book of Job many questions are raised, but the last few chapters present God as the ultimate answer. You see, God doesn't have to answer our questions; He simply *is* the Answer.

Is God worthy to be loved and obeyed even if He does not bless us materially and protect us from pain? The very character of God is at stake in this struggle. When you and I hurt deeply, what we really need is not an explanation from God, but a revelation of God. We need to see how great God is; we need to recover our lost perspective on life. Things get out of proportion when we are suffering, and it takes a vision of something bigger than ourselves to get life's dimensions adjusted again.[31]

You see, *God in His wisdom decided that it is better to bring good out of suffering than to allow no suffering to exist.*

In a world of sin and suffering God has appointed redemptive suffering to co-exist with the creatures He loves. This is nowhere more clearly seen than in the glory of the cross. That is not an oxymoron to believers—that is precious! The cross is the Grace Place where God laser-focused all of His divine attributes and humanity's weaknesses in Jesus Christ. It wasn't the miracles of Jesus that changed the world; it was His humble suffering. Nowhere is God's glory more clearly displayed in brightness and light than in Jesus on the cross (John 12:27-28). His life is the light of men.

Through Christ's death, God's attributes of holiness and justice are fully satisfied along with His great love and mercy. Through Christ's resurrection, God's attributes of power and wisdom are fully displayed along side of His grace and kindness. At the end of the day, what the world needs most is to see Jesus—the glory of God veiled in flesh, now seated at God's right hand. The cross reconciles God's love with the awfulness of human suffering.

"All things were created by Him, and for Him...so that in all things He might have the preeminence." (Colossians 1:16 & 18) He is the Most High God, and all things ultimately exist for Him and for His pleasure. Life, amazingly, does not revolve around us, but around God and His glory. Our happiness is eclipsed by God's glory and when God's glory is given its proper place—

above all else—then and only then will we find true happiness (Romans 8:18). Because we are created for His glory, when we fulfill that purpose we have fullness of joy.

So when we make much of God, honor Him, gratefully praise the wonders of His attributes, lovingly obey Him and submit to Him cheerfully, we glorify Him. We begin to understand through experience the joyful purpose for which we were created. "For our light affliction, which is but for a moment, is working for us a far more exceeding and eternal weight of glory." (2 Corinthians 4:7 NKJV) "Who is like You, O Lord, among the gods? Who is like You...glorious in Holiness, fearful in praises, doing wonders?" (Exodus 15:11 NKJV) "Be exalted, O God, above the heavens; let your glory be above all the earth." (Psalm 57:5) "I am the Lord, that is My name; and My glory I will not give to another, nor My praise to carved images." (Isaiah 42:8 NKJV)

Some have suggested that God is selfish or rather self-centered. That is a good description of us, but God is not like us. In fact, one of the greatest mistakes we could make is to think God is like us. He is not. He is the Most High—perfect and infinite in every way, totally separate from sinners; holy, righteous and good. Aren't you glad God is a good God? Try to imagine an evil God. God is good and everything He does is good. That is His essence.

Jesus said there is only One who is intrinsically good and that is God. (Matthew 19:17) He is good and upright. His goodness leads sinners along the right way. He leads people to repentance. He is good to everyone, to both the just and the unjust. "You are good, and You do good." (Psalm 119:68) He fills His creatures' hearts with food and gladness; He is ready to forgive, plentiful in mercy and rich in grace. "Taste and see that the Lord is good." (Psalm 34:8) "He works all things together for good to those who love Him." (Romans 8:28) All His works are good. It is impossible for God to do anything but good. Do you believe this truth? Do you believe God is good? Do you believe everything that comes to you is filtered through His goodness for you?

Paul wrote to the church in Thessalonica, "Therefore we also pray always for you that our God would count you worthy of this calling, and fulfill *all the good pleasure of His goodness* and the work of faith with power, that the name of our Lord Jesus Christ may be glorified in you, and you in Him, according to the grace of God and the Lord Jesus Christ." (2 Thessalonians 1:11-12) The psalmist pleads, "Oh, taste and see that the Lord is good; blessed is the man who trusts in Him!" (Psalm 34:8) When Jesus is honored and glorified in our lives we experience the joy of His goodness. We are blessed because we trust in His goodness.

Do you see how *His* pleasure is necessary for *our* pleasure? Do you also see that to glorify His goodness is not unreasonable because it brings us great pleasure and joy? God's glory in Scripture is always connected to His presence. Why? Because it is who He is, gloriously good. So "Therefore, whether you eat or drink, or whatever you do, do all to the glory of God." (1 Corinthians 10:31 NKJV) The prophet Jeremiah says it so well, "Thus says the Lord: Let not the wise man glory in his wisdom; let not the mighty man glory in his might, let not the rich man glory in his riches; but let him who glories, glory in this, that he understands and knows Me, that I am the LORD, exercising lovingkindness, judgment and righteousness in the earth. For in these I delight, says the Lord." (Jeremiah 9:23-24)

In fact, a very practical way to get a handle on the importance of glorifying God for His pleasure and our good, even in suffering, is to look at Moses (Exodus 33-34). This is vital for us because we're saying that all those human tragedies we mentioned earlier (deaths of children, missing children, rapes, divorces, injustice, including drug and alcohol abuse, abortions, verbal abuse, chronic illness, tragic accidents, etc.) have a purpose of a greater good behind them. I didn't say they were good in themselves, but we must view them in terms of God's great and glorious purpose. As we glorify God by enjoying Him we are freed from the futile despair of meaningless suffering.

Please take the time to read Exodus 33 and 34. Note that the Lord spoke face to face with Moses just as a friend would. Moses' concern was that God go with him and the Israelites on their journey. Moses prayed on the basis of God's grace and the desire to truly know Him and His ways. Grace is always needed to approach God. God answered and said, "My presence will go with you, and I will give you rest." (Exodus 33:14) Moses continues by saying that if God's presence doesn't go with them, how could anyone ever truly know and experience God's grace. God said to Moses "I'll do it—I will show grace by going with you all."

Moses' next request is most helpful to us in this discussion. "Please show me Your glory." (Exodus 33:18) Remember, God's glory is equated with His presence. Why? Because God is glorious and He is the sum of all His infinite attributes perfectly working together. Now, note God's answer to Moses, "I will show you my *goodness.*" God interchanges the words *glory* and *goodness.* God infers that to see His goodness is to see Him in all His glory. "To see My glory, is to see Me for all My goodness." Basically, God is saying, "If you were to put all My attributes together into a God-package you could call it *good* and it would be glorious!" God also says in that passage that it is His will to be gracious to whomever He desires. "So Moses, stand on that rock over there, but because you are still in a mortal body, I must veil My glory or you would die." (Exodus 33:20-23)

In that account, on the following morning, we see the display of God's goodness and glory. (Exodus 34:5-8) The Lord came down and declared to Moses His good name, "The Lord, the Lord God, is merciful and gracious, longsuffering, and *abounding in goodness* and truth, keeping mercy for thousands, forgiving iniquity and transgression and sin, by no means clearing the guilty...." Do you see anything at all here about God or what He does that is not good? Is there even one example in all of Scripture that God is not good? He is merciful and gracious—not giving us what we deserve. He suffers a long time with us patiently waiting. Then, He doesn't merely ration out His goodness and truth, but it abounds! He lavishes His glorious goodness and the reality of His truth on us superabundantly. He has withheld nothing from us. Every good gift and every perfect gift has come from Him (James 1:17).

He forgives everything in us that needs forgiving, and in case we're inclined to exceptions by unbelief, He says He forgives our iniquity, transgressions and sin. But He is also just, and will not clear the guilty who refuse His forgiving salvation.

What are all these graces, all these good things? They're the glory of His grace. Dear friend, do you realize you are a trophy on God's mantle, the mantle of His heart—a trophy of His grace? He longs for His presence, and His glory to go with us so He can bless us with His abundant goodness. Please remember that out of the darkest night, out of the travail of your soul, in your deepest depression, God is there and He is working something so good you wouldn't believe it if God told you at the time. But know that it's glorious because God is good! Would you embrace this by faith? In your trial, would you take Him for all He is and let Him bless you from the inside out? Let His love heal your brokenness. Savor, swallow, taste and see that the Lord is good. Believe, and entrust your iron-infused soul to Him as to a faithful Creator.

Remember Joseph's words to his brothers? "Do not be afraid, for am I in the place of God?" (Genesis 50:19) Give God His place; don't usurp Him. Then Joseph said, "But as for you, you meant evil against me; but God meant it for good, in order to bring it about as it is this day, to save many people alive." (Genesis 50:20) The meaning behind all of Joseph's suffering all those years was all *good*. Joseph embraced the meaning for all his afflictions in *the glory of God's goodness*.

I am convinced that as followers of Christ we are often harder on ourselves than God is toward us. Again, taste, swallow and digest God's goodness. Begin thanking Him daily and throughout the day for His goodness to you. The very best thing God did for us was sending His one and only Son to die on the cross for us. If God was so good to do that, how much more through Jesus will He also give us all the other good things we desperately need (Romans 8:32)! Never forget the goodness and blessing of His own presence in us. "Or do you not know that your body is the temple of the Holy Spirit who is in you, whom you have from God and you are not your own? For you were bought at a price; therefore, glorify God in your body and in your spirit, which are God's." (1 Corinthians 6:19-20)

To protect Moses from being overwhelmed and destroyed by God's glory he was placed in the cleft of a rock. For us, the Rock is Christ—through Him we have access to God's glory. God put Moses in the cleft and put His hand over him and covered him. God will do the same for us. But don't mistake the darkness for abandonment—it's just the shadow of the good hand of God upon us. *Glory to God in the highest and glory to God in our life!* Anything we experience has to be good if it brings us into God's presence.

> [For my determined purpose is] that I may know Him— that I may progressively become more deeply and intimately acquainted with Him, perceiving and recognizing and understanding [the wonders of His Person] more strongly and more clearly. And that I may in that same way come to know the power out-flowing from His resurrection [which it exerts over believers]; and that I may so share His sufferings as to be continually transformed [in spirit into His likeness even] to His death,... (Philippians 3:10 AMP)

Chapter 12.
The Freedom of Forgiveness

The loud knock on the door startled me. After all, it was 11 o'clock at night and we lived five miles out of town with a driveway a mile long. I was pastoring a country church. When I opened the door it was the County Sheriff. I knew what he was there for. He asked me if I would go with him to deliver a death message. They had found the son's body.

It was just after Christmas break. An extended family in our church had had a wonderful reunion in our town. The dad and mom were missionaries who had come home for the family gathering with their son and daughter plus extended family members. Well, their son had headed back to college in Texas, but never made it. His roommate had called to voice concern. Days had passed until they found his body in the bushes near the bus station. He had been robbed for about $40.00 and then stabbed to death.

When the Sheriff and I knocked on the door, the parents opened it and knew—when the Pastor and Sheriff show up it's not good. Though this kind of occurrence has repeated itself a multitude of times through the years, what happened next hasn't. Before I could say much, the father of this murdered boy took our hands and led the four of us in the most amazing prayer of heartache, forgiveness, love and hope. I was overwhelmed by their immediate offer of forgiveness toward the perpetrator. After all, he had killed their only son in cold blood.

The following week the extended family had another reunion—not so happy this time. The grief was great, but their faith was strong. The church was full. Shortly thereafter the police in Texas caught the murderer—a young man. The parents went to the trial. Between sessions the two families crossed paths. The murderer's little sister was there beside her mother and heard the conversation. The parents of the victim extended deep, heartfelt love and forgiveness to the family of the accused; after all, they had "lost" their son, too. The state of Texas was not so forgiving and sent the young man to prison for many years.

Let's fast forward—the murderer's little sister was now grown. She wrote the parents of the victim a letter and explained how, when she had heard their love and forgiveness that day at the trial, she was very moved. She had come to know Jesus' forgiveness for her. She knew the parents had continued to pray for her brother's salvation. She shared, that although he had not yet come to Christ, she visited him regularly and shared the love of Jesus with him. We don't yet know the last chapter of his life.

What we do recognize from this account is that forgiveness is a powerful force. In this lifetime, one never gets over the violent death of one's only son, who will always be dearly loved and missed. But when we know the infinite forgiveness that God, through Jesus His Son, has given us, we are able to extend forgiveness to others as well. We can trust Almighty God to take measures with justice and fairness where needed.

A good definition of forgiveness is: "Healing others by using their offenses as a means of expressing to them Christ's love."[32] Forgiveness is good for the *offender*—they experience Christ's love; and it's good for the *offended*—they experience the freedom of heart only forgiveness can bring. The opposite of forgiveness is bitterness and rejection. Bitterness is entrenched animosity, which in reality is hatred toward another person. The Greek word for bitterness is *epaza*, which means "to make fast, to fix, to fasten together, to build by fastening together." In other words, with bitterness we build a case against someone for revenge and their destruction. The English word *bitter* is closely related to the word "bite" and means—"biting, cutting, cruel." The Bible also relates bitterness to *gall*—a poisonous herb. The point is that our bitterness poisons us and everyone around us.

Forgiveness is Christianity 101 and yet it is greatly misunderstood, forgotten and withheld—and that is an understatement. I hear people all the time boasting about their bitterness and their right to be bitter. Don't get me wrong—the offense and the offender can be horribly insidious. The pain of the offense is real and can be excruciating. Note carefully here: all sinful offenses are ultimately against God. Only Jesus can forgive the *penalty* of sin—pardoning us from the eternal legal penalty of death and hell. However, we can forgive in attitude in that we show others Christ's love. When we forgive someone, we no longer wish them harm, but actually want them to experience the love of Christ and His transforming power. Remember, those parents could forgive their son's murderer from their hearts, but only the state of Texas held the power to pardon or sentence him.

God tells us, "If someone says, 'I love God,' and hates his brother, he is a liar; for he who does not love his brother whom he has seen, how can he love God whom he has not seen?" (1 John 4:20 NKJV) Jesus taught us to pray, "And forgive us our debts, *as we forgive* our debtors." (Matthew 6:12) Jesus also tells us, "But love your enemies, do good, and lend, hoping for nothing in return; and your reward will be great, and you will be sons of the Most High. For He is kind to the unthankful and evil. Therefore, be merciful just as your Father also is merciful." (Luke 6:35, 36 NKJV)

Be like your Father. Like father, like son. Focus on *His* mercy and forgiveness toward you. Love is not touchy, does not hold grudges, and does not keep a list of wrongs. Jesus taught Peter that there should be no limit to forgiveness. Remember the old saying, "He paid a debt He did not owe, because we owed a debt we could not pay."

Some years ago I heard a radio pastor say, "You should only forgive someone if they ask for it. In fact, the woman who called in was grieving the loss of her son by murder, and wanted to forgive the perpetrator. This so-called Bible teacher was greatly deceived and very wrong in his advice. He told her, "Absolutely do not forgive him since he didn't ask for forgiveness." But what did Jesus teach us? "And whenever you stand praying, if *you have anything against anyone*, forgive him, that your Father in heaven may also forgive you your trespasses. But if you do not forgive, neither will your Father in heaven forgive your trespasses." (Mark 11:25-26) If we have accepted *His* infinite forgiveness, do *we* freely forgive others?

Someone might say, "I can't forgive that person for what they did." If you are a follower of Jesus Christ, you can forgive that individual because of Christ in you. Remember, with every command for obedience, Jesus gives us a promise attached with the gift of grace. If we don't forgive, it's not that we *can't*—it's that we *won't*. Do we let His forgiveness flow through us to others? Let Jesus stand in the gap. Let Him mediate between us. When I know I need to forgive someone who has deeply offended me, it helps me to visualize Jesus on the cross for my sins.

It costs something to forgive. Forgiveness accepts the suffering; it is painful. Forgiveness knows "the fellowship of His sufferings, being conformed to His death." (Philippians 3:10) Have you experienced the fellowship of His sufferings? The forgiveness obtained for us by Jesus was very costly—but ask Him if it was worth every drop of blood. The Bible says, "And be kind one to another, tenderhearted, forgiving one another, even as God in Christ forgave you." (Ephesians 4:32)

What do we forgive? Anything we have against anyone at anytime. Joseph learned it. He forgave his evil brothers. But were his brothers off the hook with God? My friends forgave their son's murderer, but this did not absolve him from his crime against our judicial system or against God. And even if our judicial system lets us down, God will not! He is the *Supreme* Court. "Nothing in all creation is hidden from God's sight. Everything is uncovered and laid bare before the eyes of him to whom we must give account." (Hebrews 4:13 NIV)

Are you having a hard time forgiving someone who has deeply offended or wounded you? Were you molested as a child by someone you trusted? Has your spouse left you and hurt you deeply? Were you abandoned, beaten or swindled, etc.? As a follower of Jesus, what do we do with these offenses? Let me share a word picture with you that has helped me and many others. This is not a magic formula—rather it is a right understanding of our relationship with Jesus, the Truth, who is the only one who can truly set us free.

First, **look to Jesus.** See Him on the cross for you. This brings perspective. "But He was wounded for our transgressions, He was bruised for our iniquities; the chastisement for our peace was upon Him. And by His stripes we are healed..." (Isaiah 53:5-6) "For consider Him who endured such hostility from sinners against Himself, lest you become weary in your souls. You have not yet resisted to bloodshed, striving against sin." (Hebrews 12:3-4)

Second, **remove the perpetrator from your "hook"— put them on God's "hook."** We think that if we forgive someone they are "getting off the hook." But put them on a bigger hook—God's. God always writes the last chapter. He tells us, "Vengeance is mine; I will repay, says the Lord. And again, the Lord will judge His people. It is a fearful thing to fall into the hands of the living God." (Hebrews 10:30-31) The Bible reminds us, "But we know that the judgment of God is according to truth against those who practice such things." (Romans 2:2) And "the Lord executes righteousness and justice for all who are oppressed." (Psalm 103:6)

God is way more capable of dishing out vengeance because He is all powerful and all knowing. He is also totally fair— He knows all the facts from beginning to end, and He knows the thoughts and intentions of the heart. Do you believe that He will repay? Do you? When you, by faith, take your offender "off your hook" and put them on God's "hook," you are saying to God—"I am trusting You to deal with this offender. I release this offender and offense from my hook to Yours. I release with it my anger and resentment and desire for revenge."

Third, **remove your "hook" completely, and lay it at the feet of Jesus.** You say, "I forgive, but my memory of the offense just keeps coming back." Our "hook" represents our rights and expectations. We must give our rights and expectations to God. We were never meant to cling to them. This is hard for us to accept in our culture where our human rights are touted as "inalienable." The psalmist reminds us, "My soul, wait silently for God alone, for my expectation is from Him." (Psalm 62:5) Peter tells us, "Therefore, humble yourselves under the mighty hand of God, that He may exalt you in due time, casting all your care upon Him, for He cares for you." (1 Peter 5:6-7)

Look to Jesus Christ and disarm yourself—remove your "hook" that "snags" people. In fact, Jesus has really already done this for you. (See Colossians 2:13-15.) Now believe Jesus. When you relinquish your hook, you may feel a sense of loss and pain. In other words, there is a cost involved in giving up our hook.

Fourth, ***accept the sense of loss—forgiveness is costly.*** There is a price to be paid, but remember two things: first, Jesus already paid the price of forgiveness; you too are a beneficiary of His forgiveness. Second, the pain you feel in forgiving someone is always far less than the pain and consequences you'll experience if you don't forgive them.

Peter reminds us that this is our calling:

Indeed this is *your calling*. For Christ suffered for you and left you a personal example, so that you might follow in His footsteps. He was guilty of no sin, nor of the slightest prevarication. Yet when He was insulted, He offered no insult in return. When He suffered, He made no threats of revenge. He simply committed His cause to the One who judges fairly. And He personally bore our sins in His own Body on the cross, so that we might be dead to sin and be alive to all that is good. It is the suffering that

He bore which has healed you. You had wandered away like so many sheep, but now you have returned to the Shepherd and Guardian of your souls. (1 Peter 2:21-25 Phillips)

In forgiving another, whether you're feeling pain, grief, hurt, heartache, injustice, suffering, persecution—look at Jesus' hands and feet—put your finger in the nail prints, put your hand in His side. Don't be unbelieving, but believing!

You say OK, I'm willing to suffer, but the sense of loss remains!

Fifth, **let Jesus fill your sense of loss.** Let His presence flood the void of emptiness, loss, and pain. Paul writes, "But we also glory in tribulations, knowing that tribulation produces perseverance; and perseverance, character; and character hope. *Now hope does not disappoint,* because *the love of God has been poured out in our hearts by the Holy Spirit* who was given to us." (Romans 5:3-5) Now we are free to love! Paul exclaims:

And I pray that out of the glorious richness of *His resources,* He will enable you to know the strength of *the Spirit's inner re-enforcement that Christ* may actually live in your hearts by your faith. And I pray that you, rooted and founded in love yourselves, may be able to grasp (with all Christians) how wide and long and deep and high is *the love of Christ* and to *know for yourselves* that love, so far above our understanding: *So, will you be filled through all your being with God Himself!* Now to Him who, *by His power within us,* is able to do infinitely more than we ever dare to ask or imagine—to Him be glory in the church and in Christ Jesus for ever and ever, Amen! (Ephesians 3:16-21 Phillips)

What was perpetrated as the greatest offense and injustice in all of history—the crucifixion of the Son of God—turned out to be the greatest display of love and hope and freedom possible, all because Jesus is willing to forgive us! Who do you need to forgive, dear friend?

Before we end this chapter, I would like to discuss three additional issues that people often raise: *the unpardonable sin; forgiving ourselves; and forgiving God.*

The unpardonable sin. In Matthew 12:31-32, Jesus explained, "*Any* sin and blasphemy shall be forgiven people, but blasphemy against the Spirit shall not be forgiven." (NASB) Briefly put, blasphemy is defiantly mocking God. Blasphemy against the Holy Spirit is "a deliberate rejection of Christ in full light of the Holy Spirit's testimony."[33] Why is this unpardonable? Because, beyond the last testimony and conviction of the Holy Spirit there is no salvation. If you, at first, reject the testimony of God, you can hear the testimony of Jesus and the Holy Spirit and come to salvation. Many former atheists have been saved. You may have even blasphemed the name of Jesus over time and then the Holy Spirit convicts you and you repent. But after the Holy Spirit's testimony there's no witness left. Billy Graham used to say "If you think you've committed the unpardonable sin and you're concerned about it—you haven't." In other words, God is still working in your heart and you are sensitive to the conviction of the Holy Spirit. So, repent and receive His forgiveness.

The issue of forgiving ourselves. From studying this issue, it seems clear this is a modern day self-esteem concept rather than a biblical one. I think what happens is that people sin and experience guilt and shame and feel they must *forgive* themselves in order to somehow let go and move forward. But the Scriptures don't talk about forgiving ourselves. I believe what is happening is that through unbelief *we are not fully believing and receiving God's forgiveness to us.* If we go through the five steps I mentioned above, this will help us experience God's forgiveness fully. In fact, what we call *not forgiving ourselves* may be pride and self-pity in addition to not believing God has forgiven us. "If we confess our sins He is faithful and just to forgive us our sins and to cleanse us from all unrighteousness." (1 John 1:9) Do we believe this? Is God's declaration of our forgiveness sufficient? At this point the problem is not forgiveness, but lack of believing God.[34]

The issue of forgiving God. Down deep, in the midst of a long difficult trial, we secretly sometimes think God owes us an apology. "God, why me? Why didn't you stop my pain if you're God?" Sometimes, but not always, we verbalize this. Again, let me say up front, God needs no forgiving—this concept is nowhere seen in Scripture. So what's the problem?

What seems to be presented in Scripture are two kinds of offenses—one kind good and one kind bad. Jesus said: "Woe to the world because of offenses! For offenses must come, but woe to that man by whom the offense comes!" (Matthew 18:7 NKJV) Some offenses are bad and need forgiveness. Jesus was accused of not paying the temple tax, though He didn't need to, but to keep from *offending* the tax collectors Jesus paid it anyway (Matthew 17:24-27). Paul exhorted the Corinthians, "Give no offense, either to the Jews or to the Greeks or to the church of God." (I Corinthians 10:32 NKJV) Paul states, "We give no offense in anything, that our ministry may not be blamed." (2 Corinthians 6:3) And to the Philippians he wrote, "…approve the things that are excellent, that you may be sincere and without offense till the day of Christ." (Philippians 1:10 NKJV) When Peter rebuked Jesus for going to Jerusalem to suffer and die, this was a bad offense. "But He (Jesus) turned and said to Peter, "Get behind Me, Satan! You are an offense to Me, for you are not mindful of the things of God, but the things of men." (Matthew 16:21-23) Bad offenses are bad; they offend in a bad way, hurting people and undermining the testimony of God.

On the other hand, there are good offenses, or offenses that are not detrimental to people but may *offend* them to stir them to proper action. In John 6, Jesus' listeners heard a clear gospel presentation. They thought they were followers of Jesus but were not. These people complained in verse 60, "This is a hard saying; who can understand it?" Jesus responds in verse 61 "Does this offend you?" He explains the offense in verse 63-64, "The words that I speak to you are Spirit and they are life. But, there are some of you who do not believe." The gospel message offended their fleshly thinking.

In Matthew 13:53-58, when Jesus taught in His home town, the synagogue attendees "were offended at Him." Why? Verse 58 explains, "Because of their unbelief." The gospel message offended their lack of faith.

Isaiah said of Jesus, He is "A stone of stumbling and a rock of offense to both houses of Israel..." (Isaiah 8:14) Peter puts it this way:

> Therefore it is contained in scripture, "Behold, I lay in Zion a chief cornerstone, elect, precious, and he who believes on Him will, by no means, be put to shame." Therefore, to you who believe, He is precious; but to those who are disobedient, "The stone which the builders rejected has become the chief cornerstone and a stone of stumbling and a rock of offense." They stum-

bled, being disobedient to the Word, to which they also were appointed. (1 Peter 2:6-8)

There is an important and saving aspect of the cross that is *offensive* (Galatians 5:11).

Sinful man finds it offensive that he is bankrupt and can do nothing to save himself. It is offensive to free thinking intellectuals to hear that Jesus is the only way to God. There is no other way, but through the reproach of the cross. The message of the cross, calling on us to be broken in spirit, humbled, and totally dependent on God—is offensive in a saving way. There are good, right, and truthful offenses that lead us to believe Jesus' message.

So with this in mind, does God need to be forgiven? No, never! Everything God does is out of love and for our good. If He offends us, it is a good offense, not to be forgiven, but rather thanked and blessed. Matthew 11:2-6 reminds us:

When John the Baptist was in prison and heard about Jesus' great works, his faith struggled asking "Are you the coming One, or do we look for another?" Jesus answered the messengers: "Go and tell John the things which you hear and see: The blind see and the lame walk; the lepers are cleansed and the deaf hear; the dead are raised up and the poor have the gospel preached to them. *And blessed is he who is not offended because of Me."*

I know Jesus was primarily speaking of persecution, but it certainly begs the question: Does the chronic trial Jesus has left me in, offend me? We may be humbled, but are we ashamed of or offended by Him? We need to be able to say with the psalmist, "Before I was afflicted I went astray. But now I keep Your

Word. You are good, and do good." (Psalm 119:67-68) And, "It is good for me that I have been afflicted." (Psalm 119:71) And, "I know, O Lord, that Your judgments are right, and that in *faithfulness* You have afflicted me." (Psalm 119:75) Has God offended your pride and independent spirit by bringing you low with a chronic affliction? Will you trust Him for the good offenses? "Blessed is he who is not offended because of Me!"

Chapter 13.
Relationships of the Sufferer

When your soul enters the iron of chronic suffering, your relationships will be profoundly impacted. This was certainly true for Joseph. His suffering and trials had torn him from his family, completely severing those relationships for many years. His new relationships in Egypt were no doubt with people he probably would rather not have known, or at least not under those circumstances.

Every human being is relational to some degree. Some seem to be very relational and others, not as much. My wife, Denese, is extremely relational! Being with people energizes her. She has many rich relationships. I'm more in the middle. I like people, but after a while I need to retreat and recharge before engaging *with others* again. Some find themselves on the 'not-so-relational' end of the spectrum. Perhaps you're somewhere in the middle range.

As we have seen, our initial trial of suffering takes root, and then like weeds, additional trials begin to spring up everywhere. Our chronic pain begins to affect a lot of different areas of our lives—none more so than relationships. This is one reason I wanted to first deal with forgiveness in the previous chapter. When long-term adversity begins to set in, people don't quite know how to respond to us. In fact, our emotions and mental functions may be in such disarray that we don't even know what we want or how we want a relationship to proceed. These faculties we need for healthy relationships are not a mechanical thing, like putting nuts and bolts and washers together in the right order, but living and dynamic. What we need is biological, soulful, and spiritual. But when the iron collar tightens around our necks, it's hard to breathe and it's hard to communicate.

In this chapter, I'll discuss eight areas of struggle in our relationships when we're experiencing suffering. I'll refer to this connection between suffering and relationships as the 'fellowship of suffering.' In Scripture, we are given an overall command by Jesus to love one another, especially as believers. A number of 'one another' passages in the Bible also help us identify the kind of love people need. In every relationship, "what matters most is faith expressing itself through love." (Galatians 5:6) This requires a deep, gut-level trust in God while letting His love flow through us.

First, there is the struggle of "friend or foe." We see this struggle in Job's story. Job's friends started out as friends. At first, they simply sat with Job and identified with him. Words were not needed. After a week of silence they began to analyze Job's problems. As you know, this did not ease Job's suffering, but actually added to his anguish.

This friend-or-foe struggle still occurs today as well. Some people mean well, but they just don't know what to say or how to say it. The issue is not necessarily the difference between talking and remaining silent. Sufferers often simply need a quiet hug or merely the warmth of a friend's presence to know they are loved. Sometimes sufferers need words of friendship, encouragement, or admonition. The latter, however, is usually only received well in the context of a deep, caring relationship.

Because my personal illness is a mysterious and difficult-to-understand chronic pain syndrome, it is often misunderstood. I've had people say, "You look fine, what's wrong?" Others have come at me with the rebuke, "If you just had more faith, you'd be healed!" Even doctors, who were unfamiliar with my condition, told me early on, "It's all in your head." And, frankly, some people are simply mean spirited and uncaring. Most people, however, have good intentions and are sorry for us, but don't know how to respond. That's okay. We're not always sure how to respond even toward our own feelings.

Besides my dear wife, God has given me a close friend in Stan. He too suffers with a complex, difficult illness. But he understands the suffering thing and he loves Jesus. We've gotten together every Wednesday for several years to encourage each other and just hang out. Stan has been a God-send. Ours has been an encouraging, healthy relationship. Who is your Stan? Ask God for such a close friend.

No matter how people respond or react to you, let your faith in God express itself in love for others. The Bible tells us to forebear and forgive one another. (Colossians 3:13) Give people room to be who they are. Enlarge your capacity to allow God to bring all kinds of people into your life. In the end, because of Job's attitude of humility, even his three friends were restored, and Job was the better for it.

Second, there is the issue of difficult people. They are not our foes, they are just difficult! Maybe you have a spouse who just doesn't understand, or a child, who instead of helping is rebelling. Difficult people may say they love you, but loving actions are absent.

Misunderstanding is a big problem. One of our deepest human needs is to be understood. When we are not understood, this can be very frustrating. Some misunderstanding results from ignorance, and some people simply don't *want* to understand. They don't ask, and they don't care. It's especially hard when these people are Christians and should know better.

Remember too, that you don't have to explain everything or defend yourself to everyone. I know sometimes we feel compelled to, but this is another opportunity to trust God. Some people think that if you're not bleeding or have a bone sticking out of you, you can't possibly be in pain. Pain is a very subjective thing—it may or may not be visible, but it is real. I've even heard some say "I wish I could use the word cancer to label my problem, and then people would understand." I don't think those individuals actually wanted cancer; they just want to be understood.

I have read that rejection is a person's greatest fear. Maybe you've been rejected by someone, maybe even by a parent. This can be devastating, but it need not destroy us. Some rejection is conscious and outright. And, some people reject unintentionally, by not calling or checking in. In all cases, we can't control what comes to us by others, but we can control our responses.

God often allows misunderstandings and even rejection into our lives to help us lean on Him more and to help us show compassion for and forgive others. "Finally, all of you, be of one mind, having compassion for one another, love as brothers, be

tenderhearted, be courteous: not returning evil for evil or reviling for reviling, but on the contrary *blessing*, knowing that you
were called to this, that you may inherit a blessing." (1 Peter
3:8-9 NKJV) This loving activity will guard our hearts from becoming cynical toward other people.

Third there is the issue of my own problems affecting
my relationships with others. Chronic pain, whether mental,
emotional or physical can spawn other problems that affect
how I interact with others.

When we suffer chronically, we can become jealous of
others who live strong, active, productive lives. Other people
advance in school, careers and relationships, while we seem to
be stuck either on *pause*, or at least in slow motion. We may
envy what they have and secretly begrudge them.

We may struggle with loneliness or boredom, because
we can't do what we used to do. Others quit calling or stop-
ping by. They know we're not well, so they don't want to in-
trude or bother us. And we may be torn. Sometimes we wish
they would stop by, while at other times we're glad they don't
because of how we feel. So boredom sets in. The fact that our
culture is addicted to activity doesn't help either.

I have discovered as well, that many chronic sufferers experience various phobias triggered by insomnia or ill-health.
Perhaps we've become anxious. Little concerns have become
big worries and we wish it weren't so. Due to various maladies,
we may fear certain social settings. Claustrophobia has snuck
up on us and closed us in. Travel is difficult because of the un-
certainties. We get out of our highly managed comfort zone
and we panic. We experience panic attacks suddenly and with-

out warning. It puts us in awkward situations that are frightening and embarrassing. Our world becomes smaller.

Then, when people ask, "How are you feeling?" we have to size up the questioner. Is "fine" enough for now? Do they want us to tell them how we really feel? We become tired of explaining something we don't even fully understand. We experience the paralysis of analysis in terms of how to respond to others.

I'll suggest some helps in the next section, but for now, trust that God will walk through these difficult things with you. Don't over-spiritualize pain. Yes, there are spiritual aspects to it all, but pain is also a part of living in these bodies on planet earth. When relating to anyone, remember to love one another (John 13:34; 15:17). Love covers a multitude of sins and problems. Love is right in every situation.

Fourth, everyone tries to help. I could probably write a book (perhaps a comic book would be more appropriate) about all the remedies I've received through the years. Some of these remedies made good sense. Some were bizarre. Some had helped others with similar problems, and so they thought it would help me. Some were just plain nasty—just not right. Some carried undesirable spiritual implications. Some were medicinal and some were "natural". After the first four years my file was already two inches thick. I have probably received nearly 100 suggested remedies.

We must remember that most people mean well. They genuinely want us to get better. They are just trying to help. It may be exasperating for us, even confusing. Because of the financial pressures already hounding us, some can't understand why we don't try their remedy. Some actually get perturbed and angry that "we don't want to get better—if we did, we would take their remedy." They don't understand that we are all different and what works for one may not work for another.

How do we handle this barrage of advice from others? God's Word says, "Therefore, receive one another, just as Christ also received us, to the glory of God." (Romans 15:7 NKJV) Receive others. Welcome them as genuine helpers. You don't have to try everything that comes your way. Sometimes people pay for or provide the services recommended. Thank them. Be grateful. Maybe one *will* be helpful. I always tried the reasonable remedies that didn't have adverse side-effects. Even if some things didn't heal my primary problem, maybe they could benefit me other ways to add to my health. But receive these people with openness and love. Be grateful for their concern. Ask God for discernment.

Be balanced in your treatment. If controlled medicine helps, use it at least for a time, but be careful of too many overlapping drugs. Use natural remedies, but be careful to do your homework. Bathe your decisions in prayer. If you need counseling, get it. Go to someone who especially understands the spiritual side of things from a biblical perspective. It's a journey. Remember, healing ultimately comes from God in His time and His way. Sometimes you need to just back off and wait and trust.

Fifth, the issue of community. Community involves family, friends, church and others. In chronic adversity these relationships are tested. You may find out who your friends really are.

I have been blessed with an incredibly supportive and understanding wife and family. I'm not sure I'd have made it without Denese. She is a blessing from God—full of faith and joy. But that doesn't mean it hasn't been hard for her. Spouses of a sufferer suffer as much, or more, but in different ways. They stand by, pick up the slack and sometimes live very sacrificial lives in the background. They need encouragement and friends as well. Dreams as a couple may be diminished, losses accepted. Many spouses give up in these situations. My children and in-laws have been very loving and understanding. This probably means more to me than anything. The love of family is a very powerful tool.

I have also been blessed with many wonderful friends. A few have turned away and it hurts. But most have stood with us. Church has always meant so much as well. It is a community of believers journeying together. In fact, most of the rural churches I've served as pastor have suffered through much hardship and adversity. We've struggled and loved and trusted God together and it has been a great joy.

Acquaintances are different. We don't expect as much from them. It is the closer relationships of church, family and friends that can provide the biggest blessings or deepest hurts. That is why we must give our expectations to God. Maybe you have been hurt by a church or someone in a church. I encourage you to move forward. Maybe you don't have the strength to even deal with difficult people. Move on—move forward, but don't give up on the church. Jesus died for it—the church is His idea and we need each other. "Be subject to one another out of reverence for Christ." (Ephesians 5:2 NIV) Do it for Jesus! "Bear one another's burdens, and so fulfill the law of Christ." (Galatians 6:2) I've discovered that everyone is hurting in some way—we all need help.

Sixth, the issue of prayer. Someone has well said, "When we are desperate we pray." Sometimes in our desperation all we can verbalize is "HELP!" When we can't even muster that, we know that the Holy Spirit is praying for us and Jesus is interceding to the Father as well. After all these years of suffering, the reason that we are still walking with the Lord is that Jesus has been praying that our faith would not fail.

We pray because we are told to. We pray because we need God's help. Prayer declares our dependence on Him. In a mysterious, God-Sovereign way prayer changes things. We pray continually. Sometimes we can't pray. Others step in and pray for us encouraging *their* faith. One man told me his prayer life was transformed by praying for me. Praise the Lord, His prayers helped us both!

Sometimes it seems that God doesn't answer prayer. Just know that if He doesn't answer our prayer the way we ask, it doesn't mean He didn't hear it. I prayed hundreds of times for Him to take me home when the pain was too much to bear. God was silent—He didn't answer with, "Yes." In fact, all our prayers are answered—just not always as we think or wish.

I think, as God leads, we can pray for healing for others, unless God has revealed death is His plan. Perhaps mostly we can pray that people will suffer well in faith to the glory of God. I've asked for His grace to suffer well after I understood He wasn't taking me home, or healing me for now. Doesn't it make sense to ask that we suffer well?

"Pray for one another." (James 5:16) Pray for healing, but also pray for strength to bear up, to be thankful in all things—to wait on God faithfully for wisdom and timing. Pray for your character to be built up; that your faith would strengthen and persevere; that people would see Jesus in you; that you would bear up by His grace and glorify Him in all things. Maybe more than anything else—suffering teaches us all to pray.

Seventh, the ministry of comforting others. At first we may not even want this ministry, but I believe the longer we suffer and find our comfort in God, the greater our capacity to comfort others. We are reminded, "Blessed be the God and Father of our Lord Jesus Christ, the Father of mercies and God of *all* comfort, who comforts us in all our tribulation, that we may be able to comfort those who are in any trouble, with the comfort with which we ourselves are comforted by God." (2 Corinthians 1:3-4)

The above is so true. In my trouble, I have been comforted by other people in ways not even fully known to them. God has comforted me in very personal ways. I am comforted by the mercy of God the Father. I am comforted by the victory of Jesus, and I am comforted by the Comforter, the Holy Spirit. I have seen people become very comfortable in their relationship with God through their deep suffering. Others experience discomfort, but never yield their situation to Christ and they don't experience the comfort of God. When personal intimacy with God is absent, a vacuum of hopelessness rushes in.

God is attracted to weakness. He comforts those who are downcast. We have a God who has suffered. Our High Priest suffered more than anyone. He knows your pain. He stands by to personally comfort you. Our trials aggravate, annoy, exasperate, perplex, torment, torture and dog us. But when we allow God to comfort us personally, through His Spirit, and through others, the peace of God arrives—the pleasure of His company alleviates these trials. There is a contentment and rest that He brings. He consoles and assists us. He restores our soul;

He compensates with Himself; He shows us pity and compassion. When we are hindered, hurt, injured, and annoyed, He consoles, bolsters our courage, invigorates our spirit, calms our storm, and leads us by still waters.

God used the lives of some of the prophets, like Ezekiel, as "signs" or living lessons of truth. Sometimes your comfort in God is a sign to an unbelieving world. We are told to "comfort one another" (1 Thessalonians 4:18) and we can only do that when *we allow God to comfort us*. Are we allowing Him to comfort us?

Eighth, the struggle of meaningful service. Since we've already covered this subject, I want to put a twist on it. I suggest that we, as sufferers, actually have an advantage over the healthy. Though trouble can complicate some things, in many ways life is simplified, because we just don't have the energy or ability to do what we once did. Think of the quadriplegic or the one whose eyesight is lost. Adversity has a way of simplifying and clarifying life. Suffering can help us focus on the most important issue—our relationship with God and others. But, in order to accomplish anything relational, *we need a certain amount of daily routine*. Without establishing and sticking to some simple, healthy, daily practices we will not be able to cultivate the relationships we so sorely need. Sadly, many sufferers have given up on life and their relationships. Instead, they sleep, drink, or medicate their days away.

I cannot overstate the importance of simply getting up in the morning, using the bathroom, taking a shower, eating breakfast, reading our Bible, and doing what we need to do to prepare ourselves for the day. We need to run errands, make a phone call, get the mail, take a walk, etc. We should do whatever we can to move through the routine of a day trusting God to guide us and make meaningful contacts as we go. Take baby steps; plan a picnic or some other outing; develop a routine, and be flexible. If you're having a rough day—thank God for His presence and comfort and start again tomorrow. But, get up, get dressed and live the day with the strength God gives you.

As part of our daily routine, we need to "Serve one another." (Galatians 5:13) It has long been understood that the most helpful thing someone can do for their own well-being is to serve someone else. Service for others may be through words, actions, a touch, a hug, or a prayer. Your service may look different than that of a healthy person's. Your service may simply be the profound action of a smile through your pain.

Remember, at the end of the day, *what the world needs most to see is Jesus.* Serve others Jesus. Partner with the Holy Spirit. Share your life. Attend a small group. Just live life and do it as Christ gives you strength. If you have a bad day, God understands. Again, *what matters most is faith expressing itself through love.* Love God and love others.

Chapter 14.
Magnification—Overcoming Fear

I first noticed it in the dimly lit car. I couldn't read the map. My declining eyesight was sudden and frustrating. I was told this curse would take effect on my 45th birthday and now it was here. I reluctantly went to the store and picked out my first reading glasses. I needed magnification.

Praise the LORD for magnification! With magnification, I had a new perspective on small objects. It gave me clarity and focus. What is interesting about magnification though, is that the objects don't actually become bigger; they just *appear* larger. Magnification is the process of enlarging something only *in appearance,* not in actual physical size. But magnification can be either helpful or harmful. FEAR is one such magnifier in life.

Fear makes things *appear* much bigger than they really are. Fear intensifies a situation and enlarges the problem. Fear is impressive in its ability to lead us to places we would not normally go. An example of this phenomenon is found in Deuteronomy 28. God warned Israel against leaving Him for other gods. He warned that leaving Him would make their worst fears reality. They would have no rest. Instead, they would experience: "A trembling heart, failing eyes, and anguish of soul; your life shall hang in doubt before you; you shall fear day and night and have no assurance of life. In the morning you shall say, 'Oh that it were evening!' And at evening you shall say, 'Oh that it were morning!' because of the sight which your eyes see." (Deuteronomy 28:65-67)

I think what God was saying is that reality will be bad, but their fear will magnify its effects. Yet, His warning was to keep them from sinning. This reminds us then that there are two kinds of fear—good, healthy fear; and destructive, exaggerated fear. We learn early in our childhood not to touch a hot burner. We develop a healthy fear or respect for heat. That fear, or respect, keeps life normal and healthy. But there is an unhealthy fear that causes an individual to recoil and isolate themselves in their home like a prison. This fear is exaggerated and unhealthy and keeps us from normal activities that we would otherwise enter into.

In this chapter I want to present three concepts: unhealthy fear, healthy fear, and the process God gives us to overcome unhealthy fear.

First, let's look at unhealthy fear. This emotion takes what you know, what you think you know, or what you may actually be experiencing and magnifies it. To the degree that you let it, fear can become very disabling. When I first became ill, one of the most frightening things for me was that sleep fled from me immediately. Like the flick of a switch, I lost my ability to sleep. For weeks, I slept perhaps only one hour a night. I couldn't nap. It was as though I was drugged awake.

Because of my responsibilities and what sleep deprivation does to one mentally, I became frightened. I couldn't believe this was happening and I couldn't stop it. Nothing helped at first. Then weeks without sleep turned into months. All of a sudden, little things turned into giants. Little things I could've handled in the past without thinking became insurmountable. My mind exaggerated problems and distorted my thinking. Have you been there? What fears do you struggle with because of your chronic trial? Another fear that plagued me was, "Will this ever end?"

Destructive fear can take a real experience and inflate it. We can point to a real problem that has actually happened. Fear doesn't deny the original problem. I had a severe kidney stone—it was very real and painful. But then for a time, I let my imagination run away with me about possible future kidney stones. "What if I get a kidney stone attack when I'm in a crowd? What if I'm on a plane as another one strikes?" We start the *what if* cycle. Fear feeds our imaginations and scenarios begin to loom much larger than the original problem. Our perspective of reality changes because we have imagined *hypothetical* situations that often don't seem to be solvable.

There appears to be two disabling results with destructive fears. One result is that my fear looms larger than the reality of my situation. In other words, my fear has become irrational. The second result is that my fear magnifies problems to become monstrosities bigger than God can handle. Even though my mind may *know* certain things to be true about God, my imagination seems to gain the upper hand.

When our boys were eight and ten, they had vivid imaginations. One night we had a young teenage girl, who was a friend of the family, watch our boys. The boys imagined hearing a burglar outside trying to get in. They frightened the babysitter with their imagined scenarios to the extent that she locked them all in the bedroom; was holding a butcher knife for protection; and called us in great fear. The boys weren't trying to scare her, but their imaginations got the best of them all.

We called a neighbor to go check on them and there was no burglar—all was well. Needless to say, she never babysat for us again!

When our imaginations kick in, we visualize an image in our mind or heart. These images can be creative or destructive. When based on reality, imaginations can be creative—like designing a new car. But when imagination lacks reality, it becomes a fanciful, empty (and usually destructive) assumption. In fact, we define imaginary as "void of truth." When fear grips our hearts we can imagine all kinds of crazy things.

Maybe you remember a little kid's book called *The Great Big Terrible Whatzit*. The book was designed to help little kids overcome their fears; fears like going down to the basement. The big monstrous furnace belched and moaned, and growled, and looked ominous. As the story unfolds, and the child understands the true nature of the shapes and noises, the monstrous furnace becomes smaller and smaller until it isn't so scary anymore.

I know of some women who are afraid of *all* men because of a hurtful divorce they experienced. We shouldn't deny or belittle the difficult situation, but have we let fear project an image far beyond reality? A friend of ours is a single woman who was a missionary in Africa. One evening three men broke in to her home, beat her up and robbed her. Few of us have experienced something so horrifying. As a result of her experience, fear understandably became an issue for her. Yet, through a process of time and trust in God, she has overcome her fears, and has become a healthy, productive person. I don't think we ever get over some things or totally eliminate fear, but we do learn to conquer it and overcome it when it rears its ugly head.

The second kind of fear is good, healthy fear. I see two
categories of this kind of fear. One category of healthy fear
prompts us to take protective measures to avoid injury or dam-
age. When I ride a motorcycle, for instance, I wear a helmet for
protection. I'm fond of my head and want to keep it intact. Protective measures provide safety nets and are reasonable. We
might say they involve a healthy respect for danger and seek
to avoid or minimize painful situations. We wear safety goggles
and oven mitts. We lock our doors and pay our taxes.

A second and more important category of healthy fear is
the wholesome fear of God. Because of who God is, the Most
High God, we hold Him in profound awe and reverence. For the
follower of Christ, the fear of God is the worshipful acknowledgment of our accountability to Him. The Bible is replete with
examples and exhortations on the fear of God. God is to be our
fear and dread. Godly fear is for our good—it keeps us close
and accountable to Him. "The fear of the Lord is the beginning
of wisdom" and knowledge (Psalm 111:10). "The fear of the
Lord is a fountain of life," which brings happiness and is clean
and endures forever (Proverbs 14:27). We are told to "Serve the
Lord with fear and rejoice with trembling." (Psalm 2:11) The fear
of God is the deep respect and reverence we creatures should
have in healthy relationship with our Creator. In fact, Acts 9:31
connects two things we don't often equate: "Walking in the
fear of the Lord *and* in the *comfort* of the Holy Spirit." To choose
to fear the Lord is not only right, it is comforting. "The fear of
the Lord is to hate evil." (Proverbs 8:13)

Jesus brings this subject to focus in Matthew, "And do
not fear those who kill the body but cannot kill the soul. But
rather, fear Him who is able to destroy both soul and body in
hell." (Matthew 10:28) Our greater fear of God overcomes and
dispels our lesser fears. We were taught not to enter someone's

house without their invitation. Yet, when my brother saw our neighbor's house on fire and could not get a response from knocking, his lesser fear of intrusion was overcome by his greater fear of harm coming to our neighbor and he barged in to alert them. John reminds us:

> Love has been perfected among us in this: that we may have boldness in the Day of Judgment; because as He is, so are we in this world. There is no fear in love; but perfect love casts out fear, because fear involves torment. But he who fears has not been made perfect in love. We love Him because He first loved us. (1 John 4:17-19)

Perfect love, the kind God has for us, casts out the tormenting fear of judgment. Praise the Lord!

So, is there a practical way for us to overcome unhealthy fear? I believe there is, since what God commands He enables. We've already seen two helpful ways to overcome unhealthy fear: fearing God (the greater) to overcome our lesser fears; and believing—taking a hold of—God's incredible love for us. With these two ways of overcoming unhealthy fear in mind, I would like to share what I believe is an incredibly freeing truth to enable us to be more than conquerors when it comes to fear.

Paul told Timothy, "For God has not given us a spirit of fear, but of power, and of love, and of a sound mind." (2 Timothy 1:7 NKJV) God has not left us to overcome our fears by our own effort or even using the right "tools." The entire Godhead, the triune God: Father, Son and Holy Spirit are with us to help us. This verse also seems to imply that there are "spirits" of fear out there. But a follower of Jesus has not been given that spirit of fear. Instead, we have God's Holy Spirit, who is the Spirit of power, love and a sound mind.

The Holy Spirit doesn't just give us power, love and a sound mind; He *is* these things to us. He empowers us to overcome fear by strengthening us through His presence in our inner being. He also pours His love into our hearts, reminding us of how much and how good the Father and Son are to us, especially since Jesus already gave His all for us. Knowing and experiencing God's love are powerful antidotes for fear. Then the sound mind instructs us. As the Spirit of truth He speaks truth and spiritual reality to our minds. He literally shares with us the mind of Christ, full of grace and truth.

We've been given a God-sized helper, the Holy Spirit. The process of overcoming fear is a lifelong battle, in which fear is defeated and replaced with a loving trust in our Heavenly Father. The Holy Spirit transforms us from the inside out. The Holy Spirit's ongoing work in us gives us new perspective. The Holy Spirit accurately shows us that God is bigger than any of our problems, fears or anxieties. He keeps things real. He corrals our thoughts and helps us "take captive our thoughts into obedience to Christ." (2 Corinthians 10:5) The Holy Spirit does not allow us to deny the reality of the trial we are experiencing. He simply applies the lens of truth to see the greater reality in our situation—the spiritual reality of God's powerful, loving mind. The Holy Spirit empowers us to visualize and experience the love of Jesus for us.

Over and over in the New Testament Gospels, Jesus told His disciples "Fear not;" "Trust me." After the disciples frantically woke Jesus, who was sleeping in the back of the boat in spite of the storm, Jesus asked them, "Why are you so fearful? How is it that you have no faith?" (Mark 4:40 NKJV) Jesus equated believing God with overcoming fear. Do we believe God in specific situations of fear? It's hard to trust someone we don't know very well. Is God "the blessed controller of all things," or not? Does He not work all things together for good for those who love Him? (Romans 8:28)

Finally, let's look at the key to overcoming fear. We'll find this key in a very unlikely place, the virgin birth of Jesus. Even before the multitude of heavenly hosts proclaimed, "Glory to God in the highest, and on earth peace, goodwill toward all men!" we see it. (Luke 2:14 NKJV) Before we continue, I would encourage you to read the biblical account of the virgin birth to help you understand this vital truth. (See Luke 1:26-56.)

We have said that one way to overcome fear is to fear the greater God. We have also said that fear is a magnifier; it causes us to perceive things as larger than they are. With this in mind, note that when the angel Gabriel appeared to Mary, she was *troubled* by or *afraid* at his presence. So, Gabriel comforted her with the words, "Fear not, Mary." (Luke 1:30) Later, in response to Gabriel's pronouncement, Mary proclaims what is called her *Magnificat*. There, overwhelmed by God's work and favor upon her, she expresses, "My soul magnifies the Lord, and my spirit has rejoiced in God my Savior." (Luke 1:46-47)

Consider with me what's going on here: Jesus, a member of the Trinity, the very God who created Mary's womb is now humbling Himself to enter her womb as a baby! He, whom Mary magnifies has humbled Himself to become a man and "became obedient to the point of death, even death of the cross." (Philippians 2:6-11) Jesus, as God, became a man and *de-magnified* Himself for our salvation and God's glory. Then, God the Father *magnified* Him by *highly exalting* Him and giving Him "a name *above* every name on earth or in heaven." Consequently, "every tongue will confess that Jesus Christ is Lord, to the glory of God, the Father." The writer of Hebrews urges us, "Consider him [Jesus] who endured such opposition from sinners, so that you will not grow weary and lose heart." (Hebrews 12:3 NIV) In other words, considering who Jesus is and what He has done for us, what or whom shall we fear?

In Mary's Magnificat, she showcases at least eleven attributes of God for all to see His magnificence. Notice, in this case, God isn't made to appear bigger than He is; Mary simply brings into focus for us just how awesome He is. There is a magnification of God's significance to Mary's soul and spirit. She rejoices and makes much of God by elaborating His attributes. "In providing a Savior, You have displayed Your great grace. By regarding me, a lowly maid-servant, You have shown Yourself to be very personal. By implanting the Son of God in my womb, You have declared Your power and sovereignty."

"You have displayed Your holiness in Your holy name. You have been merciful to many generations. You have a strong arm in Your display of justice. You are righteous by exalting the humble. You advertise Your goodness by exercising it everywhere. You are faithful and You are
eternal."

"Praise God from whom all blessings flow. Praise Him all creatures here below. Praise Him above ye heavenly hosts. Praise Father, Son and Holy Ghost."[35] Fear not, for I am your God! Making much of God in praise and worship quickly dispels our fears. I praise the name of the Lord Jesus Christ! It's all about Him. He must increase and we must decrease.

The Psalms are a great help to us here in conquering our fears. The psalmists are real. They transparently share their fears and concerns, but they always conclude in praise and exaltation to God. Magnifying God has a very powerful faith-effect over disabling and debilitating fears.

Luke also reminds us of God's promises to us. Shortly after Gabriel's pronouncement to Mary, she visited her cousin Elizabeth. When Elizabeth saw Mary, she exclaimed, "Blessed is she who believed, for there will be a fulfillment of those things which were told her from the Lord." (Luke 1:45) Mary was blessed or happy because she believed what God told her. Do you believe what God has promised you? What specific promises has God given you in your chronic trial? Do you believe God will complete His work in you; bless you; see you through; provide for you; protect you; forgive you; care for you; comfort you and strengthen you?

One of the most encouraging things I've done in the past few years of my trial is to write down promises of God—personal words from God to me to help sustain me. I know we want to apply His Word appropriately, yet God speaks to us through His word in very personal ways and wants us to apply His Word to our lives. (Romans 15:4)

Following are some examples of God's promises we can cling to as our own: Philippians 4:13; 1 Peter 5:7; 2 Corinthians 2:14; Isaiah 40:28-31; Isaiah 41:10; Romans 8:1,28,37; Psalm 115:14; Psalm 18:31-32; 81:10; Matthew 14:27; Proverbs 3:5-6; Hebrews 13:5b AMP; Isaiah 64:4; 63:9; 1 Peter 5:10-11; John 11:40; 2 Chronicles 20:15-17; Matthew 19:26 Psalm 37:5,7; 46:10; 55:22; 2 Corinthians 12:7-10, etc.

Better than any promise is Jesus Himself! Gabriel encouraged Mary, "Behold, you will conceive in your womb and bring forth a son, and shall call His name Jesus." (Luke 1:31) Matthew adds: "…for He will save His people from their sins." (Matthew 1:21) To be able to call upon the name of Jesus in times of fear is priceless. The Godhead: Father, Son and Holy Spirit work together to help us through those fearful times. As a follower of

Christ you are never alone. Do not be afraid. Speak peace to your heart in Jesus' name. Believe His word. Embrace His promises and magnify Him above all. Recognize that God is bigger than your fears, infinitely bigger.

Dear friend, Scripture reminds us, "Do not be afraid (*your name*), for you have found favor with God." (Luke 1:30) His Word promises us, "For with the Lord nothing will be impossible"—even overcoming our fears. (Luke 1:37) Declare to God as Mary did, "Let it be to me according to your word"—even the pain and suffering of a chronic trial. (Luke 1:38) Do you believe God can conquer your fear? Talk it out with your Deliverer. Speak truth to your heart. Above all make much of God. Magnify, exalt, lift up, glorify, praise, honor, speak highly of, and worship Him extravagantly! "God is our refuge and strength, a very present help in trouble. Therefore, we will not fear." (Psalm 46:1-2) "Be still and know that I am God; I will be exalted [*magnified*] among the nations; I will be exalted [*magnified*] in the earth." (Psalm 46:10) Be still my heart and know your God. See Him high and lifted up magnified above all my fears.

"Yet in all these things we are more than conquerors through Him who loved us." (Romans 8:37) To conquer is to overcome my fears, to be more than a conqueror is to be loved by God and so to delight in and make much of Him. Give thanks! Be grateful! Accept His love! Don't look for merely the absence of fear, but the filling of God Himself. You are an overcomer! You are a fear-conqueror through Jesus Christ! Accept God's love. Be comforted by the Holy Spirit. Recognize God as great and impressive. Intensify your view of Him. See Him as He is—magnificent!

Chapter 15.
Hope against Hope

Someone once told me, "Cheer up. Things could be worse." So I cheered up—and, by golly, things did get worse! In the dynamics of chronic pain, hope is vital. But when you've tried every conceivable cure to no avail, despair begins to move in like fog. Things grow dark and confused. We sometimes lose our bearings. Hope slowly disappears and we begin to lose heart.

Most of us have probably experienced the debilitating effects of hopelessness. This underscores the great need in our human experience for hope. Without hope it's nearly impossible to go on. But with hope, a person with incredible, seemingly insurmountable odds against them can not only continue, but do so joyfully. I think of Nick, the Australian evangelist who has no arms or legs. Yet he works full time, eats, dresses, swims and travels the world over speaking to tens of thousands encouraging them in the faith.

Not all hope, however, is created equal. There is human hope, and a divine hope. There is a natural, generic hope that we attribute to the human spirit, but there is a supernatural hope that only God can provide.

First, there is the hope most people think of—a desire that what we want will come to pass. I may say, "I hope the Mariners win their double-header today." I have a positive outlook because they've been winning, and I want to see them win. The probabilities of their winning may be good because they've won two-thirds of their games this year. Perhaps they also have the best pitching statistics and the team they're playing hasn't done that well. So, will they win both games? I hope they will. Yet, I really can't say for sure. I certainly wouldn't bet my life on it. I hope it won't rain tomorrow. I hope my investments do well this year. I hope my grandkids are all born strong and healthy. But for all my hoping, I have no guarantees.

There is also the human hope that we talk about as "the power of positive thinking." This brand of hope recognizes the importance of our mental attitude towards achieving a goal. We speak of "psyching oneself up" for participating in a sports competition, or "believing in ourselves" as we venture out in a new business. And while there is something to be said for a positive mental attitude, the chronic sufferer needs firmer ground.

Contrast human hope with divine, biblical hope. Divine hope is a certain, for sure, know-it's-so hope. I can take it to the bank. This hope is firmly convinced of better things ahead, a happy anticipation of good, but it's more. Biblical hope is confident expectation in God's ways, means, ends and timing. Its ground or basis is God Himself. Hebrews 6 reminds us that God is immutable or unchangeable. He means what He says and says what He means. He has made statements of promise to those who will take Him at His word, and He never lies. In fact, it's impossible for Him to lie because He can't contradict His own character—truthfulness.

This divine hope involves three things: 1) promise, 2) anticipation, and 3) fulfillment. First, God has made profound *promises* to us. If we obey the Gospel we will be saved from His wrath and experience eternal life. Once we obey the Gospel, all the good promises of God open up to us. Paul reminded the Corinthians, "But as God is faithful, our word to you was not 'Yes' and 'No'. For the Son of God, Jesus Christ, who was preached among you by us—by me, Silvanus, and Timothy—was not 'Yes' and 'No', but *in Him* was 'Yes'. For all the promises of God in Him are 'Yes', and in Him: Amen, to the glory of God through us." (2 Corinthians 1:18-20 NKJV)

All the promises of God to followers of Jesus (i.e. those "in Christ") are positively a resounding "Yes!" He promises, "I will never leave or forsake you. I will love you unconditionally. I am coming back for you. I will work all things together for your good and my glory. I will give you love, joy, peace, patience, etc. I will; I will; I will." All the promises and divine orders are stamped with a big "Yes!" What a sure hope! In this hope we receive supernatural strength in our trials. Someday our trials will end. The future joy is infinitely greater than the present pain. "Embrace Me," Jesus says. Flee to Me as a refuge of hope—see Jesus clearly—let Him give you a bigger perspective on your trials.

Know too, that hope will never disappoint. We are encouraged, "Now hope does not disappoint, because the love of God has been poured out into our hearts by the Holy Spirit who was given to us." (Romans 5:5) I must confess here that this verse bothered me a few years into my chronic trial. I *was* disappointed. I *had* hoped in God, or so I thought. My circumstances just never improved. My soul was parched, and my hope wavered—until I remembered the love of God that is better than life itself. The Holy Spirit turned on the faucet and I drank my fill and kept going back to drink.

You see, at first my hope had been for a change of circumstances. And when nothing changed, I began to lose hope.

But when I realized that my hope is based in God's unending, extravagant love for me, *I* began to change. God wasn't disappointed in me, nor I in Him. How could I be disappointed? I'm loved by God. How could He be disappointed in me? He sees Jesus in me.

I began to thank the Holy Spirit for ministering God's love to me. I also began to understand that hope undergirds my endurance. Lest I get blown away by the trials of life, hope anchors my soul. "This hope we have as an anchor of the soul, both sure and steadfast, and which enters the Presence behind the veil." (Hebrews 6:19) Unless we are anchored by hope in the immutable God we will be driven by the winds of adversity, and tossed up and down on an emotional roller coaster. And if we're not careful, it may take us where we don't really want to go.

I think when Joseph was collared in prison and his soul entered the iron, the Holy Spirit ministered love and life to him. I think Joseph did what Peter admonishes us to do, "Therefore, gird up the loins of your mind; be sober, and rest your hope fully upon the grace that is to be brought to you at the revelation of Jesus Christ." (1 Peter 1:13) Because I am anchored in the grace of Jesus, when God completes my trial, the ultimate promise of deliverance will be heard in heaven—"Yes!"

This introduces us naturally into the *second* thing this good biblical hope involves: *anticipation*. Again, we see a time element in our faith journey. At the conclusion of the love chapter, Paul says, "And now abides faith, hope, and love, these three; but the greatest of these is love." (1 Corinthians 13:13) A few years ago Denese was in an airport waiting for a flight when she looked over and saw Bob Hope standing by himself. Well all she had with her to write on was her Bible, so she walked over and asked him for his autograph. He agreed and signed it. Well, I always thought he should have written under his name, "And now abides faith, hope, and love, but the greatest of these is Hope." J Why does love stand out as greater than faith or hope? Because right now, as we anticipate the coming of Christ, we need all three. But when we see Jesus, faith and hope will be realized, and only love will be needed. Love is eternal. Faith and hope joyfully anticipate that day.

Dear friend, as you struggle through your adversity, let me bless you with a blessing from God: "Now may the God of hope fill you with all joy and peace in believing, that you may abound in hope by the power of the Holy Spirit." (Romans 15:13) The source of all hope is God, and by the provision of His Spirit He wants you to *abound* in hope—not just get by. Positive people see the glass half-full. Believing people see the glass full and running over. In this verse we see a great definition of hope: "joy and peace in believing." Hope involves trust in God which results in joy and peace.

When we say we trust in God, we are also saying we are placing our hope in Him. Like peanut butter and jelly, trust and hope go together. When you believe God you are hoping in Him. As we trust Him hope fills our hearts.

Believing God always brings joy. Joy is the happiness, pleasure, gladness, delight and enjoyment we experience when we are in right relationship with God. Therefore, trusting God enables us to find pleasure of soul in Him even though pain is present. Believing in Jesus, we are reconciled to God. And through Jesus, we tap into the powerful ongoing joy produced exclusively for us by God's Spirit. Joy originates from God. It's a spiritual fruit and is greater than my circumstances. Do you believe that? Do you believe that joy already abounds like a bubbling fountain in your heart? "He who believes in Me, as the Scripture has said, out of his heart will flow rivers of living water." (John 7:38) Peter calls it "a living hope"—personal and from God Himself. Joy is sharing in the happiness of the Trinity. We don't have to manufacture it. Joy is a living gift to each of us. As a believer, it's in you already to the full. Take advantage of it—enjoy God—believe with the joy of good expectation. Anticipate God's goodness and love. Hope again!

Not only is there joy in believing, there is also peace. God's peace is "that tranquil state of a soul assured of its salvation through Christ, and so fearing nothing from God and being content with its earthly lot of whatever sort that is..." (Philippians 4:7 AMP) Though my soul is collared by the iron of affliction, it is also content because it is at peace with God. As we anticipate the fulfillment of our hope, Jesus is our peace. He has removed the enmity, or hostility which I previously had with God because of my sinful rebellion.

Before I believed in Christ, I had no hope, was without God in this world and far away from Him. But now, through Jesus' sin-bearing on the cross I am brought near to God by the wrath-satisfying blood of Jesus. God is no longer angry or at odds with me. He is for me—I stand acquitted, forgiven and fully cleansed. Where sin left a hole, God rushed in with joy and peace and gave me hope. I now have a tranquil soul. He has killed the panic. I enjoy the peace of God through Jesus. I no longer fear God's judgment. I am assured of a love relationship with God through Jesus. The Holy Spirit ministers peace to my soul so that even if I experience tribulation in this world, I can cheerfully know—Jesus in me has overcome the world.

So, as I believe in Jesus—all that He is, for all that I need— I have hope. This hope is a God-provided hope, full and bubbling over, powerfully supplied to me by God's Spirit residing within me. This is a hope that is full of joy and peace in believing.

> That is, as I trust my life to God, as I am convicted and convinced that God not only exists but that He is my Creator, and so He sovereignly rules over every detail of life, providing everything I need and blessing me with eternal salvation through Jesus Christ. I can then lean my entire human personality on God in absolute trust and confidence in His power, wisdom and goodness. (Hebrews 13:7 author's paraphrase based on the Amplified version of the Bible.)

My hope comes from God—it is grounded in the Father, made possible by Jesus' work, and ministered to me by His Holy Spirit. All this is promised and recorded for me in His word. So, this divine hope is not just wishful thinking, but a joyful and peaceful belief that embraces true spiritual reality.

So, we've talked about the promise of hope and its anticipation. The *third* aspect of divine hope is: *fulfillment*. For hope to come from God, there has to be a favorable outcome—a good ending. If anticipation of a promise is believed, then fulfillment must be realized. If we are firmly convinced of better things based on God's promises, then the better things "must" come.

Many who read this, who are in the trenches of a long chronic trial, will actually see your trial end within your lifetime. We all know of people who have been healed of long-standing illnesses. We know of people who have overcome deep, long-term emotional hurts through the grace of God. I had a rare bone disease in my early years that God resolved through a successful surgery.

However, I am presently struggling with a chronic pain disorder that I've had now for 15 years and there's no end in sight. But here's where the third aspect of divine hope comes into play. Whether the illness will be removed in *this lifetime* or not, I don't know. What divine hope assures me of is the fact that my illness will be removed, for certain, in heaven. "And God will wipe away every tear from their eyes; there shall be no more death, nor sorrow, nor crying. There shall be no more pain, for the former things have passed away." (Revelation 21:4 NLT)

Peter reminds us of this ultimate hope that saturates the pages of Scripture. "So think clearly and exercise self-control. Look forward to the special blessings that will come to you at the return of Christ." (1 Peter 1:13 NLT) Do you look forward with great anticipation to the coming of Christ? For me, the return of Christ is and has been vital for my spiritual and mental well-being. Paul reminds Titus that we live "in hope of eternal life which God, who cannot lie, promised before time began." (Titus 1:2 NKJV)

It is important to note that the moment we are born again, we have eternal life, which is the very life of God. We enter His life in both quantity and quality. Eternal life *starts for us in this lifetime*. Having said that, the Scriptures also speak of *looking forward* to eternal life—this means the new life, with new bodies we will experience after death. So there is a sense in which we now have eternal life and then we will someday enter into the full experience of it. In the present we are given the precious gift of hope.

Once again Paul encourages Titus with these words, "Looking for the blessed hope and the glorious appearing of our great God and Savior Jesus Christ." (Titus 2:13 NKJV) I can't even express in words what this "blessed hope" of Jesus' return means to me. As the weeks, months and years of the fog of pain fully set in, my prayer was, "God, please take me home!" I just wanted the pain to stop! God said, "Not yet, for my grace and hope are sufficient for you!"

God's response led me to a long journey of studying the prophetic Scriptures, which make up at least 28% of the Bible. I discovered that the prophetic Scriptures are some of the most encouraging and practical portions of the Bible. Perhaps you've heard it said that the death of a Christ-follower makes heaven a little sweeter (if that were possible). For years now, I often wake up in the morning and look out the window and ask, "Is today the day of your return, Lord Jesus? Will You be coming back today?" Then I go about my day with a God-consciousness and watchfulness filled with comfort and hope.

It is amazing to me how many Christians are not actively looking for the coming of Christ. I can hardly wait to see my Savior and fall on my knees and thank Him for His great love and sacrifice on my behalf. Please don't fear Christ's return or be afraid of Bible prophecy! Prophecy is as much a part of God's Word as John or Romans. All of God's Word is necessary and profitable. *Revelation* means to *reveal* or *unveil*. What is Revelation unveiling? Two primary themes: God's plan for our future and the glory of Jesus more fully disclosed. What could be more hope filled?

Paul wrote to the Corinthians, "If in this life only, we have hope in Christ, we are of all men the most pitiable." (1 Corinthians 15:15 NKJV) Why is this? Because, in this world we will be inundated with tribulations, persecution and suffering, but for hope to be divine hope there needs to be a good expectation and fulfillment. Jesus was able to bear the cross because of the future joy of many brothers and sisters joining Him in the family of God. This is a resurrection hope—a life-born-out-of-death hope. John reminds us of the angel's word at the end of the Bible, "And he said to me, 'Do not seal up the words of the prophecy of this book, for the time is near.'" (Revelation 22:10)

There are two swings of the pendulum of prophecy that throw us out of balance: first, those who set dates for the return of Christ; and second, those who dismiss prophecy as unimportant. A proper balance of understanding prophecy is to put Jesus squarely in the center. We need to study prophetic Scriptures diligently; seek the Holy Spirit's help for understanding; believe God's Word and then obey it. I believe that much of the hopelessness of our day is due to a lack of understanding the basics of prophetic Scripture. Paul said, "I have hope in God, which they themselves accept, that there will be a resurrection of the dead, both of the just and the unjust." (Acts 24:15 NKJV)

So, dear friends and companions in suffering, know that *hope* is our great tool and weapon to triumph over difficulties. Consider our great role model, Abraham, "Who, contrary to hope, in hope believed, so that he became the father of many nations, according to what was spoken, "So shall your descendants be." (Romans 4:18 NKJV)

God had called Abraham out of his homeland to a new and different place. God made promises to Abraham of a land and a "seed" or descendants. Between the giving of the promise and the fulfillment of it, God leveraged that duration of time as a tool of faith in Abraham. God used *lapse of time* to build faith, hope, anticipation and other character traits vital to His plan for Abraham. This was because Abraham's relationship to God was more important than anything else.

The Bible says God waited until Abe was about a hundred years old—his body as good as dead for fathering children. Also, Sarah was old and her womb was well beyond the age of childbearing. Theirs was now an impossible situation. Had God forgotten His promise? Was hope dead too? Yet it says of Abraham, "Contrary to hope, in hope he believed." (Romans 4:18 NKJV) At first glance, this sounds like double-talk. But what it means is that circumstances were contrary to the hope he'd been given. Like us, circumstances of chronic adversity over time, cry out against the reality of God's good promises to us. Our reality may look like this: nothing is getting better—we're in an impossible situation physically, financially, emotionally, relationally, and spiritually. We see no way out or even through our trials. We see God's promises to us, but reality shouts a different scenario!

Well, when all human hope is gone, God's gift of hope still stands. God never changed. He can't lie. His promised reality is greater than my present circumstances. I need to wait in hope and glad expectation for Him. I know this can be quite challenging for us. It is intended to be. We question the very core of our faith and hope, and well we should. God is not afraid—His Word stands true. Test it, dear ones.

The Romans 4 context gives us some further insights. Abraham's situation was desperate—He needed a resurrection. Then we are told, "He did not waver at the promise of God through unbelief, but was strengthened in faith, *giving glory to God*, and being fully convinced that what God had promised He was also able to perform." (Romans 4:20-21) At times we all have doubts or mental hurdles we must overcome, but we follow in the footsteps of the faith of Abraham our father. That is, we trust and hope in God.

Let me conclude this chapter with this: when our life circumstances seem contrary to hope, we must continue to believe God through His divine hope. Don't be fooled by circumstances—don't be fooled by time frames. Be fully convinced in your heart that God will carry out His promises to you. If your hope has taken a hit, hope again. Give glory to God.

We need a bailout, a stimulus package—His name is Jesus. Hope rests in grace for the long-haul. Hope makes the painful place the hiding place of Jesus. Hope provides the stamina for the long suffering.

- A resurrection hope brings life out of death.
- A promised hope brings future fulfillment.
- A righteous hope brings conformity to God's will.
- A Gospel hope brings good news of great joy.
- A glorious hope makes much of God.
- A blessed hope brings a happy ending.
- A saving hope gives an assuring protection.
- A knowledgeable hope brings a personal appointment and invitation.
- An eternal hope brings a full and realized life.
- A living hope brings relation and animation.
- A better hope brings Jesus our high priest.
- An anchoring hope brings staying power.
- A purifying hope actively cleanses.
- A completing hope makes us diligent to the end. And…
- A convenient hope is accessible and renewable.

PRAISE THE LORD!

(The above points are taken from: Acts 23:6; 26:6,7; Galatians 5:5; Colossians 1:23; Romans 5:2;; Titus 2:13; I Thessalonians 5:8; Ephesians 1:18; Titus 1:2; Acts 28:20; II Thessalonians 2:16; I Peter 1:3; Hebrews 7:19; 6:18,19; I John 3:3; Hebrews 6:11; 6:18.)

Chapter 16.
Getting it Right

What do you believe about God and where did you get your information? The answer to this question goes to the core of your soul. In the quietness of your soul, long after it has entered the iron of suffering, who has God revealed Himself to be?

When I was pastoring a wonderful country church in Paradise Valley, Montana, we would meet outdoors in an amphitheater of log pews at the KOA next to the Yellowstone River. We would hold our summer Sunday morning services there to enable campers to have a place to meet. The owners of the KOA, who are dear friends, would hire foreign students to work for the summer. One young lady was the daughter of a Muslim cleric in Indonesia.

After weeks of her being drawn in by the worship music, she finally sat in the service. Denese and I invited her over to dinner shortly thereafter. She told us she enjoyed the service, but had to ask Allah for forgiveness for attending. Soon into the evening she made a provocative statement. She said, "Your God is the same God as mine." Politely I said, "Tell me about your God. What is he like?" I wanted to hear it from a devout follower's own mouth.

For the next few minutes she described her god as very distant and difficult to know. She said Allah tricks people, so he is hard to read and trust. He changes his mind, so his will is hard to know. After listening for a few minutes, as kindly as I could, I said: "The God of the Bible, Jehovah, the God and Father of the Lord Jesus Christ is very different from Allah." I told her that "Jehovah is very near and seeks a personal, love relationship with us. He never tricks us or leads us into evil. He has clearly revealed Himself and His will and intention for us in the Scriptures. He never wavers—He is the same yesterday, today and forever. I can depend on Him." Then she said, "Well, I guess they are two different gods."

This led into a two hour discussion about Jesus Christ. Denese and I explained the gospel of Jesus Christ to her in a variety of ways. Finally a light came on in her eyes and she said, "So what you are telling me is that Jesus took my place on the cross and died for my sins—He's paid for all my sins and offers me total forgiveness and a relationship with God Himself—and all I need to do is repent and believe Him?" I said, "Yes, that's it." She said, "If that were true that would be the greatest news. But it's too good to be true." I said, "It's so good because it *is* true!" When I asked her what would happen if she returned home a Christian she told us, "I'd be killed, like many other Christians in my village." At least she left with an understanding of the Gospel. We pray she truly believes it someday.

I believe that though our country has Judeo-Christian roots, many Americans now worship a different god. From listening to our culture today, I would say that America now believes in the "god of their own opinion." We have reinvented a god in our minds from a smorgasbord of opinions.

What does all this have to do with chronic suffering? Obviously, our eternal destiny is at stake, but *what we believe about God determines the answers to our questions about suffering.* Our culture and its opinions have lowered our view of God.

Popular thought has made Him more "manageable." But is that correct? Is that even helpful? No, absolutely not!

In this context, A. W. Tozer has said a lot of things well:

- "The low view of God entertained almost universally among Christians is the cause of a hundred lesser evils everywhere among us."
- "What comes into our minds when we think about God is the most important thing about us."
- "No religion has ever been greater than its idea about God."
- "We tend by a secret law of the soul to move toward our mental image of God."[36]

Whether we've thought about it or not, we all have a personal statement of faith. What do we really believe? Do we get our information about God from our culture, our own opinions or other's opinions, or do we get it from the revelation of God Himself in His Holy Scriptures?

As a young man, I went on a canoe trip in the Boundary Waters Canoe Area of northern Minnesota. I'll never forget when my close friend stepped out of the canoe onto a lily pad, thinking it was a rock. As he pulled himself out of the lake, we all had a good laugh. Fortunately, my friend could swim and other than a damaged ego and wet clothes, his experience was harmless and funny. But when we attempt to find firm footing on the "lily pad" of our own ideas about God, the stakes are infinitely more serious. On what are you standing? Are you standing on the solid rock of God's revealed Word, or on the "lily pad" of your own God-concept?

A statement of faith summarizes the essentials of what one believes. What do you believe about God? How does your statement of faith affect the way you process your pain? Suffering moves the great universal questions of life down to a very personal level because pain is very visceral and personal. Chronic pain has entered my soul—and has begun to define my life. Do you know from God's revelation to us in the Scripture who God is? What are God's answers to the questions:

- Where did I come from?
- Who am I?
- What defines my identity?
- Why am I here? (This answers whether my suffering has a worthy purpose.)
- Where am I going?
- What does God require of me?
- What has God provided for me?
- How does He communicate with me?
- What is wrong with the human race?
- What is wrong with me?
- What am I willing to die for?
- What am I willing to live for?
- How do I reconcile suffering and pain with all of the above?

Many people today have a very distorted view about truth. A cartoon I saw recently demonstrates this confusion around truth. The caption said, "The lies behind the truth, and the truth behind those lies that are behind that truth." Do you see this muddled thinking? A comedian coined the word "truthiness." Does that mean there is some truth to it, but that it's not *pure* truth?

Does God mean what He says, and say what He means? I often hear people object that we can't really know the Bible, because so many take it so many different ways. Is that thought accurate, or is it that we don't really believe God's Word? Are there many opinions because God is vague and has not clearly spoken, or is it because we impose our own views on the Bible interpreting it to our own liking? Or are the variations of views simply the result of sloppiness, poor study habits, unbelief, or disobedience? D. L. Moody used to say "Obedience leads to knowledge." If we come to Scripture with the intention to obey it, no matter what, then chances are we will understand it. But if we come to the Bible for knowledge with a wait-and-see attitude, and then decide whether we want to obey it, we open ourselves up to confusion, deception and rebellion. Faith is taking God at His word.

Don't you think that if God had a saving message for mankind regarding the gracious provision of the death of His Son, that He would make that message clear and preserve it for us? I think so! As a sufferer, does it matter to us if God is intrinsically good? You bet it does! Would it make a difference to us to know that God is absolutely sovereign in all life's issues and that He is all powerful—that He could stop or start anything—that He could heal or give us grace to endure? Would it change our life to know that an infinite, eternal, all-knowing God loves us with a perfect and overflowing love? Would it help if we knew He proved His love beyond question by putting His Son through incredible torture and death just for us? If we knew that God always keeps His promises—would that encourage us to persevere? And even when we didn't understand much of anything about our trial, would it make a difference to know God is infinitely wise? Is the greatness of His own majesty worth our pain—is it worth the glory He deserves? Is a temporary affliction, even perhaps for a lifetime, worth eternal glory in the presence of God? What do we believe about God? Let us state our faith and then by God's grace let us live in it.

What difference does God make in our lives? Does our faith display integrity? In other words, does what we *say* we believe translate into *how we live?* Are we willing to entrust our souls to God as a faithful Creator? If Jesus is our Lord, then doesn't He, by right, have complete authority over us, His servants, to do as He pleases? If God is our Father, then shouldn't we be subject to Him willingly and lovingly?

The prophet Elijah stood before the people of Israel at Mt. Carmel and confronted the prophets of Baal, exposing their foolishness. Elijah challenged Israel, "How long are you going to waver between two opinions? If the Lord is God, follow Him! But if Baal is God, then follow Him!" Then note the people's response, "But the people were completely silent." (1 Kings 18:21 NLT) We could ask ourselves that question today, "Are we wavering between two opinions? If the Lord is God will we follow Him and reject any other false god of our imaginations?"

As believers who are suffering chronically, are we wavering between believing God or believing our own, or someone else's opinion? Are we unstable and double-minded? Are we like the people of Israel who were completely silent? In Elijah's day, Israel sat on the fence—a very uncomfortable place to be. They couldn't or wouldn't make up their minds. The point is: a decision must be made. Who or what are we following? Are we following a religion, our professors, our parents, our friends, our own heart, our culture, the majority, a philosophy, a view, or an opinion? Or, are we decisively, with abandonment, following our Creator who loves us?

Today we are told any and all religions lead to God. The Scripture states that there is only one way to God—through Jesus. The conclusion we must come to then, is that religion is simply different ways of *rebelling* against God. What we need is a *Declaration of Dependence.* The fact is we are all dependent on God, whether we realize it or not. Who will we follow and depend on?

Everything we have is a gift received from God. Paul reminds us: "For who makes you differ from another? And what do you have that you did not receive? Now if you did indeed receive it, why do you boast as if you had not received it?" (1 Corinthians 4:7) Job said it this way, "Naked I came from my mother's womb, and naked I shall return there. The Lord gave, and the Lord has taken away; blessed be the name of the Lord." (Job 1:21) Oh, that we would bless God for His gifts as much as we complain about our losses. Paul said, "For in Him we live and move and have our being." (Acts 17:28) Paul also reminds us that God has no needs. He is complete in Himself and, "He gives to all life, breath and all things." (Acts 17:25) God is the great giver of every good and perfect gift. We are the *recipients* of His gracious hand—even the unwanted companionship of a difficult trial. The apostle James encourages us:

> When all kinds of trials and temptations crowd into your lives, my brothers, don't resent them as intruders, but welcome them as friends! Realize that they come to test your faith and to produce in you the quality of endurance. But let the process go on until that endurance is fully developed, and you will find you have become men of mature character, men of integrity with no weak spots. And if, in the process, any of you does not know how to meet any particular problem he has only to ask God—who gives generously to all men without making them feel guilty—and he may be quite sure that the necessary wisdom will be given him. But he must ask in sincere faith without secret doubts. For the man who doubts is like a wave of the sea, carried forward by the wind one moment and driven back the next. That sort

> of man cannot hope to receive anything from the Lord, and the life of a man of divided loyalty will reveal instability at every turn. (James 1:2-8 Phillips)

We balk at our dependence on God because of our pride. We like to think we are strong, independent people. But we are not—we are quite weak and dependent. God's grace, the very thing we need most in our trial, is the thing we resist in stubbornness and pride. A dependent person is a humble person. Humility is acknowledging our helplessness and God's helpfulness. Someone once told me, "You Christians just use God as a crutch." Well, not only is He my crutch, but my wheelchair, hospital bed, ventilator, IV and doctor! The truth is I was dead in my sin and needed a resurrection. He is my very life. James continues, "But He gives more grace. Therefore He says: God resists the proud, but gives grace to the humble. Therefore, submit to God. Resist the devil and he will flee from you." (James 4:6-7 NKJV)

Do you suppose that a person feels helpless when a medic zaps him back to life with a defibrillator? Yes, but it saves his life. Why in the world would we ever resist God's help of breathing new life in us during our deepest trials?

I write these things to myself as well. Since we're all dependent on God (whether we acknowledge it or not), let us knowingly, willingly and gratefully submit ourselves to His help. Let us go deeper in our humility to drink more deeply of His grace. Is your trial breaking you? Dear friend, your faith relationship to God is what's at stake. Your faith is a very precious thing to God. Someone once said, "A wound is the quickest way to the heart."

I know chronic pain is a battle. It's like being severely wounded in battle, but still having to fight. Faith *is* a fight. Faith is the fight of our lives. Faith is being tested at the gut level and even the sub-gut level. Paul reminded Timothy, "Fight the good fight of faith, lay hold onto eternal life." (1 Timothy 6:12) Your belief system is under attack. The attack comes from three fronts: the world, the flesh and the devil. The anchor of hope is being torn at. The devil wants to steal, kill and destroy you. The world, like a heavy weight, is pulling you down. Your heart struggles with deep issues. Your mind is attacked by fear, imaginations, destructive arguments and prideful thoughts against God. Our hearts condemn us. Wave after wave of adversity crash down upon us. The enemy throws fiery darts of lies and half-truths at us. "Yet in all these things we are more than conquerors through Him who loved us." (Romans 8:37) The battles may rage, but the war has been decided. It's like watching a ball game on replay when you already know who won. Even though they are down 4 to 0 in the seventh inning, you already know they score 5 in the ninth to win. For a time it may look bleak, but you know the outcome.

Some of us need to believe our way back to God. I don't mean you weren't saved, but in the heat of the battle you've lost ground because of doubt. Believe again! "Trust in the Lord with all your heart and lean not to your own understanding; in all your ways acknowledge Him, and He will direct your path." (Proverbs 3:5-6)

This battle of faith is different than other battles. Our weapons are mighty and spiritual. We focus not on the enemy but on Jesus. We look to Jesus, the Author and Finisher of our faith. When we suffer we're tempted to keep our eyes on ourselves. Instead, look up! Look to Jesus! He knows. He has been through your pain. "Who for the joy that was set before Him endured the cross." (Hebrews 12:2 KJV)

Dear friend, when I lose my bearings I refocus on the cross of Jesus. At the cross, pain is refocused. At that cross I have the clearest proof that God cares for me. Suffering was given to Jesus by God so that He would glorify God by overcoming it. Jesus saw past the pain to the pleasure of honoring God and bringing to Him many sons and daughters to behold that gracious glory. Jesus overcame pain by finding and receiving pleasure in His Father, and so can we. At the cross, all the attributes of God are laser focused. At the cross, I see the lowest level of humility, and the farthest reach of grace. At the cross, I see God does care. He is for me. I have reason to go on and finish the fight.

> He was despised and rejected by men, a man of suffering who knew what sickness was. He was like one people turned away from; He was despised, and we didn't value Him. Yet He Himself bore our sicknesses, and He carried our pains; but we in turn regarded Him stricken, struck down by God, and afflicted. But He was pierced because of our transgressions, crushed because of our iniquities; punishment for our peace was upon Him and we are healed by His wounds. We all went astray like sheep; we all have turned to our own way; and the Lord has punished Him for the iniquity of us all. (Isaiah 53:3-6 HCSB)

As I focus on Jesus, I see the image of the invisible God, the brightness of His glory. I see the Compassionate One who gave it all. I see the Patient One waiting for me. I see the Relentless Pursuer pursuing me. I see Jesus, not riding the fence but jumping it in decisive action, saying, "Father, if it is Your will take this cup away from me; nevertheless, not My will, but Yours, be done." (Luke 22:42)

So here's the crux of the matter, "For as the sufferings of Christ abound in us, so our consolation also abounds through Christ." (2 Corinthians 1:5) Where sin abounded grace does much more abound. Where suffering abounded the coming glory of being in God's presence totally out-paces and out-distances and out-weighs all my pain. Jesus has given us two privileges: "For to you it has been granted on behalf of Christ not only to believe in Him, but also to suffer for His sake." (Philippians 1:29) He's also called us to a moment of truth. "Whoever desires to come after Me, let him deny himself, and take up his cross, and follow Me. For whoever desires to save his life will lose it, but whoever loses his life for My sake and the gospel's will save it. For what will it profit a man if he gains the whole world, and loses his own soul? Or what will a man give in exchange for his soul?" (Mark 8:34-37)

Jesus says to us, what is the exchange rate? What exchange is worth giving up our soul? Jesus, through the Gospel, says, "You give Me your soul, your life with all its sin and failure and weakness, and I'll give you My life—eternal life, and My righteousness that enables reconciliation with God the Father. It will cost you your present life, for you must lay it down with the same decisiveness I exercised at Calvary. You must tell God—'Not my will but Your will be done.'"

Paul summarizes our life in Christ like this, "I have been crucified with Christ; it is no longer I who live, but Christ lives in me; and the life which I now live in the flesh I live by faith in the Son of God who loved me and gave Himself for me." (Galatians 2:20) Win-win living. What an exchange! He gets me and I get Him. Praise the LORD!

I end this chapter asking again: Who do you believe God to be and where did you get your information? What is your statement of faith? What do you really believe? Would you die for your belief? Are you willing to wait for your ultimate healing? Maybe you're like the Father in the story of Mark 9 who said to Jesus, "Lord I believe; help my unbelief." (Mark 9:24) God will meet us where we are and even help us believe. What a God!

Chapter 17.
Let the Worshippers Arise

A few years ago, while living in an apartment on medical leave, I had an interesting conversation with a neighbor. This young family was a delightful bunch. He was attending university, his wife was Asian and well educated, and they had a beautiful baby. We had many good conversations about God. One day as we were talking about Jesus, he was agreeing with most of what I said, yet I could tell he really didn't entrust his life to Him. In an effort to clarify his relationship with Jesus Christ, I said, "Because of who Jesus is, God in the flesh, we must worship Him." This is where my friend fell short. He said, "I believe in Jesus, but I don't see Him as one to worship." As kindly as I could I said, "Then you don't really believe Him or know Him because to believe who He is and what He said and did is to worship Him." To refuse to worship Jesus Christ is to miss Him completely. When we come to know Jesus in a personal, intimate way we are compelled to worship Him.

Jesus told the woman at the well that the Father is seeking "true worshippers" because "true worshippers *will* worship the Father in spirit and in truth." (John 4:24) This means that believers, born of the Spirit, will worship Him. True worship is based on relationship with God at the spirit level and on the truth of who Jesus is. Based on God's revealed truth, worship is a person's desire and response to seeing Jesus as He truly is, the Most High God.

We have the privilege of worshipping God willingly from the heart in a way that honors and glorifies God. Paul reminds us that ultimately everyone will bow the knee to Jesus, "Therefore, God has highly exalted Him and bestowed on Him the name that is above every name, so that at the name of Jesus every knee should bow, in heaven and on earth, and under the earth; and every tongue confess that Jesus Christ is Lord, to the glory of God the Father." (Philippians 2:9-11 ESV) Someday, even if my neighbor does not now believe and worship Jesus as Lord, he will bow the knee and acknowledge Him as Lord at Judgment Day. It's just that it will be too late for his salvation. Even now the demons believe Jesus; they know who He is yet refuse to worship Him. Ultimately the whole universe will bow in submission to Jesus Christ.

Yet, knowing now who Jesus is and what He did to purchase our salvation—why wouldn't we willingly and gladly worship Him? Even in the midst of incredible, misunderstood suffering, our best response should be worship. There is great wisdom in worship. It helps us get and keep our hearts anchored and right before our Creator. True worship brings focus and magnification on God and humbles our hearts making them receptive to His infinite grace.

I think of Job, who in one day lost his children, many of his servants and his herds. So in one day he lost his family and his livelihood in terrible tragedy. Yet, note Job's initial response, "Then Job arose and tore his robe and shaved his head and fell on the ground and *worshipped*. And he said, 'Naked I came from my mother's womb, and naked shall I return. The Lord gave, and the Lord has taken away; blessed be the name of the

Lord.' In all this Job did not sin or charge God with wrong." (Job 1:20-22) How many of us worship God as our initial response to great personal tragedy?

I believe Job's example is a call to every believer—"Let the worshippers arise!" In fact, I believe that as we read the Bible and observe life, our best response, and sometimes the only response, is simple, humble, heartfelt worship. In all of life, our most fitting response is to acknowledge that God is the Most High God, all-knowing, all-seeing and all-wise. We can trust Him. In fact, when you think about it, maybe suffering brings us great advantage. In a very profound way, suffering simplifies and clarifies our most basic relationship, our relationship to our Creator. In fact, if I cannot worship God, especially in a time of great tragedy, I do not really know Him. He is worthy of all worship because of who He is and what He did for me in sending His own Son to suffer and die for my sins.

The psalmist reminds us, "Before I was afflicted I went astray, but now I keep Your word." (Psalm 119:67) "It is good for me that I was afflicted, so that I might know your statutes." (Psalm 119:71) "I know, O Lord, that your rules are righteous, and that in faithfulness you have afflicted me." (Psalm 119:75) "If your law had not been my delight, I would have perished in my affliction." (Psalm 119:92) "Trouble and anguish have found me out, but your commandments are my delight." (Psalm 119:143) Do you agree with the psalmist?

Early on in my trial when I lost my strength and stamina and pain moved in, I was devastated because of how little I could do. My activity level dropped to a slow-motion survival mode. I thought, "What can I do? What meaningful occupation and service can I render to others, or even to God?" Then the Lord reminded me of heroes of the faith like Job who simply worshipped God. Or what about a quadriplegic who can't move, or an elderly woman in a nursing home who still loves Jesus but has so little strength? I realized that every one of us can worship God—anytime, anywhere, and under any circumstances.

Before our trial, when all is well or at least running somewhat smoothly, we are busy and distracted. Many things occupy us. What I've learned, though, is that worship is *the* most worthy vocation. It is the *ultimate* use of time. To be still and worship God is never a waste of time. The worship of God is our highest calling. And chronic suffering especially helps clarify worship for us. Worship of God is the very purpose for which we were created. I remember a young woman in a worship service praising and worshipping God like I'd never seen. Her worship was over-the-top jubilant and she was refreshing to be around, yet she had been mentally challenged from birth. Her mind was limited, but her spirit wasn't. In my chronic illness, I began to take opportunity throughout the day to consciously worship God. This practice changed my perspective, brought meaning to my life and honored God.

But for many, I believe, worship seems mysterious. What in the world is worship? Early on I asked myself that question. After meditating on it for some time, reading what others said about it, and saturating my mind with the Scriptures, I began to make a list of what worship is. In short, worship is bowing before the Most High God and honoring Him for His worth. As we have seen, worship is a heart issue from the spirit and done in truth, since God requires truth in the inward parts. Worship can also be prompted by a specific experience or occasion as it was with Job. When I delivered to the parents the news of their son's murder, they stopped right then and there and prayed and worshipped God.

Yet, worship is not limited to an action we would describe as prayer or praise, for worship is a lifestyle as well. When we are worshipping God all week, as a way of purposeful living, the Sunday morning hour is just an extension of our worship. I'll bet Job had a lifestyle of worship long before tragedy struck. What is in our hearts expresses itself through our mouths. A heart full of worship will express worship vocally. So, worship can be manifested through words of praise or through song. Music is one of the most pleasure-filled forms of worship, and is very edifying to the church body. Music is a gift from God, which we are able to give back to Him in worship.

Our bodies are instruments of worship as well. Paul tells us, "I appeal to you therefore, brothers, by the mercies of God, to present your bodies as a living sacrifice, holy and acceptable to God, which is your spiritual worship." (Romans 12:1) So, because we are a whole person, we may raise our hands or bow our knees in worship. Yet the act of submitting our body to God in holiness is also a lifestyle of worship through sacrificial living. Many today forget that this living sacrifice, obedience to God, is as much a part of worship as a praise song in church. We can show worship in our attitudes, during the day, in our suffering. Whatever we do, we should do as an act of worship to the glory of God—whether serving, giving, working, or even just resting. Most of all, we are worshipping whenever we find pleasure in God and enjoy Him. Here is my list of what worship is. Can you add to it?

Worship is:
- The only legitimate response to Almighty God, our Creator and Redeemer
- The response of my heart that brings the greatest pleasure to God's heart
- My deepest humility for His Highest Glory

- The glad devotion, passion and obedience to my Lord and Savior
- The only true response to the One who loves me with perfect love
- My appropriate response to the Greatest Gift
- The very purpose for which I was created
- The ultimate human aspiration
- The joyful celebration when my focus is on Jesus
- My HIGHEST calling—Most worthy vocation—Ultimate use of time
- The one thing that God desires from His creatures that brings both Him and them the most intimate pleasures
- The eternal occupation of Heaven
- The great necessity for entrance into Heaven
- The Garden of Grace that produces the fruit of praise, adoration and glory
- The cry of the preciousness of the cross
- The sweet surrender of the will on the Altar of Grace
- The only adequate response to the Holiness of God
- The praise of the glory of His Grace
- Declaring worth to the Worthy One
- The reason I'm still on the earth
- The acknowledgment of my healthy fear of God
- Reveals my identity—who I really am
- The ultimate rest in His Ultimate Work
- The cry of a soul set free from sin
- The sufferer's submission to His sovereign God

Sometimes when I'm hiking in the woods I am overwhelmed with a sense of God's presence. Sometimes I'm awestruck in silence—I can't even speak. Silence can be a form of worship. Other times I break out into a praise song, or simply begin to tell God how much He means to me and how much I love Him. Sometimes I worship God with my attitude during a particularly difficult time of pain or exhaustion. Psalm 100 tells us to serve the Lord with gladness. At times, even when we don't feel like it, we obey and honor God with a sacrifice of joy and gladness. And other times we don't feel like we have anything to give Him at all in worship except our pain. Remember, in your faith relationship of being "in Christ," there is a fellowship in His suffering. We share in His suffering and He shares in ours. The apostle John wrote in the first chapter of Revelation, "I, John, your brother and partner in the tribulation and the kingdom and the patient endurance that are in Jesus." (Revelation 1:9)

Jesus Christ shared in our pain on this earth and ultimately on the cross. Only by faith do we share in His pain. "I am crucified with Christ." Also, through the suffering of persecution, as a follower of Jesus, I may suffer, bearing His reproach through identification with Him. Yet, only *His* pain and suffering can save me. And even though the cross is a finished work of salvation, Jesus continues to work as my High Priest, interceding on my behalf.

Ultimately, what I'm saying here is that when it seems all you have left is your pain, offer it to Him as a spiritual sacrifice of worship. He does heal the broken hearted. When we honor God, even in the midst of unwanted, unbelievable, and unending pain, this is a sacrifice of worship. If your jar of clay has been filled with pain—pour it out as an offering to God. Then let Him fill you with Himself. The spring of living water will restore your soul and will never run out. As the writer of Hebrews expresses, "Through Jesus, therefore, let us continually offer to God a sacrifice of praise—the fruit of lips that openly profess his name." (Hebrews 13:15 NIV)

Let your life, dear friend, be one defined and characterized by worship. Make it your highest aspiration to worship the God and Father of the Lord Jesus Christ. Spend and expend your time on this earth doing it. Do it with the strength, as little as it may be, that you've been allowed. If you can't move your lips, praise Him with your thoughts. If your thoughts are foggy, praise Him with your spirit. If your heart is too hard, let the hand of the Potter soften you up through your pain. Let God mold your worship. Trust your pain to God. As Jesus turned water into wine, let Him turn your pain into His pleasure through worship.

Some people worship work or sports or whatever idol they have set up in their lives. Such pursuits consume them and their time. How about us? To cultivate a worshipful heart takes time. Let God consume your thoughts. Let His Word saturate your life. Be consciously aware of His presence. Talk to Him about everything. Exchange worry, anxiety, complaining and grumbling for worship.

For many of you, like me, worship may be hard to grasp. Let me share with you some thoughts that have helped me on my journey. The starting point for worship is that Jesus is our mediator to God, the Father. All worship to God the Father must initiate through Jesus, the name above all names. Apart from Jesus we would have no access at all to the Father. Without Jesus our worship would be tainted and fruitless. From this perspective, all worship must be done in and through the matchless name of Jesus. "For there is one God, and there is one mediator between God and men, the man Christ Jesus." (1 Timothy 2:5 ESV) God, the Holy Spirit helps us in all these things. He is our Comforter and the Spirit of Truth. He constantly points us to Jesus for the Father's glory. He also prays for us.

Having said that, here are some practical ways to help us worship God:

First, Scripture provides *worship words* that teach us how to honor God: words like *praise, exalt, extol, magnify* and *glorify.* Use these words from your heart. *Boast in* and about God. *Adore* Him, *applaud* and *appreciate* Him. *Cheer* and *compliment* Him. *Recognize* and *pay* Him *tribute. Cry out in devotion* and *esteem* Him *highly. Give thanks; be grateful. Celebrate* and *make much of* Him. *Eulogize* and *elevate* Him. *Rave* about Him. *Revere* and *bless* His name. Use these words. Cause His name to be lifted high. After all he is your awesome God, infinite in splendor, incredibly imposing, beautiful and breathtaking, majestic and magnificent, overwhelming, mind-blowing and stunningly wonderful. He is our God. Think it, say it, mean it and sing it, and play it and live it.

Second, worship God for His specific attributes. Contemplate His *holiness:* His sinless perfection; He is above and separate from sin; He is perfect in practical holiness; He is *righteous* and operates righteously in everything. Praise Him for His *transcendence:* He is above all others by infinite degrees; and He is mysterious and yet has revealed Himself to us. "The secret things belong to the Lord our God, but the things that are revealed belong to us." (Deuteronomy 29:29 ESV)

Thank God that He is *immutable:* He never changes, therefore we can always count on Him. Worship Him for His *power.* Bless His *wisdom.* Adore His *mercy.* Recognize His *righteousness.* Pay tribute to His *justice.* Applaud His *omniscience.* Appreciate His *omnipresence.* Cheer His *sovereignty.* Celebrate His *providence.* Boast in His *creativity.* Honor His *truth.* Extol His *goodness.* Glorify His *grace* and *love.*

This is who God is. Worship Him personally. Recognize how He is different than we are. Get in Scripture and learn who He is. Be detailed. Don't make Him something He is not. Let His character stand, and seek to understand what He has revealed about Himself. Let the mysterious and inscrutableness stand. God is bigger and more wonderful than we could ever imagine!

Third, worship God in the *names* by which He reveals Himself. His names identify the vastness and unity of His person. From Almighty God and the Great Jehovah, to the I AM and Father in Heaven, to the many names of Jesus that describe who He is. He is:

- Alpha and Omega
- Our Advocate
- Blessed and Only Sovereign
- Chosen of God
- Friend of sinners
- Immanuel—God with us
- Head over all things
- Messiah
- The Holy One
- Innocent and Undefiled

Praise His name as:

- The Hope of Glory
- The Image of the invisible God
- The Judge of the living and the dead
- The Lamb of God
- King over all
- The Lawgiver
- The Light and Life
- The Bread of Life
- Lord of Glory

- The Lord our Righteousness
- Merciful and Faithful
- The Word of God
- Wonderful Counselor
- Almighty God
- Our Peace
- The Resurrection and the Life
- Our Savior
- Servant
- Son of the Most High
- Stone of Stumbling
- The Teacher
- The Truth
- The Way
- The Life
- The Wisdom of God
- Our Shepherd
- Our Rock
- The Door

Remember, His name is high and lifted up, and at His name every knee will bow and every tongue will confess Him as Lord.

Delight in who He is. Take pleasure in Him as a friend, who is closer than a brother. Revel in and entertain thoughts of who He is. Know the thrill of relationship with Him and relish His presence.

Fourth, worship the Lord for His *works*. Thank God and enumerate the blessings of your salvation. Show gratefulness for your justification and forgiveness. Bless Him for your ongoing sanctification. Show appreciation for His providence and protection and provision every day. Celebrate the victory you've been given in Christ. Be awestruck by His creativity. Look at the stars and see the glory of God's handiwork. Study anatomy and see the wonders of His design. Some of the Psalms focus on His works. You can see how worship of this sort can honor God and also teach us much. "Come and see the works of God; *He is* awesome *in His* doing toward the sons of men." (Psalm 66:5 NKJV)

Fifth, worship God for His *words*. Because God is truth, His words are true and right. I may say, "I'll meet you at 10:00 am," and then forget. God doesn't forget. He always keeps His Word. Love and study the Word to see your God. Speak His Word back to Him in praise. Use the Psalms. "O Lord, our Lord, how majestic is your name in all the earth!" (Psalm 8:1 NIV)

Revelation also has some wonderful words of praise. "You are worthy, our Lord and God, to receive glory and honor and power, for you created all things, and by your will they were created and have their being." (Revelation 4:11 NIV)

Be diligent and be consistent. Take Him at His word. And remember, Jesus is the Living Word, and the Holy Spirit is the Inspirer and Teacher of the Word. Bless Him for that.

So let the worshippers arise. Are you a worshipper? Arise and shine and give God the glory.

> Praise God from whom all blessings flow.
> Praise Him all creatures here below.
> Praise Him above ye heavenly host.
> Praise Father, Son and Holy Ghost.[37]

"Bless the Lord, O my soul." Someone may say, "I don't feel like worshipping." Well, as a pastor once wisely said in response, "You don't have that right." God deserves our worship because He is worthy. Obedience in worship can change our feelings and can change everything about us!

Worship that is rendered through pain is precious to your Savior. A sufferer has a special responsibility and a special advantage. Give Him glory through your pain. He is worthy and you'll be blessed.

Chapter 18.
Your Defining Moment

Well, we've covered a lot, but there's a lot we've missed. Maybe you have been able to relate to much of what we've discussed. Again, this book is for those whose pain never really goes away. Your soul has entered the iron. The collar is tight around your neck—it's hard to breathe. Life is different, very different for you. Whatever your pain, it is real and it has set up residence in your life. You hope for relief and closure in the land of the living, but you know it may not come this side of heaven.

You didn't ask for your chronic affliction; it is an unwanted calling laid upon your life. You have struggled with the "why" questions just like Job. You've recognized that there are mysteries in life that simply aren't answered. Yet, in your pain you've gone back to what you know about God and how He works as He builds our faith. You've begun to understand the wisdom and value of waiting on God. You've been challenged to become a "believing believer" truly taking God at His word in the daily grind. We've seen that the health of the universe is the holiness of God. We learn to enter into His holiness for true spiritual health, which is of infinite importance.

Then we've camped at the Grace Place—the place in Christ where we receive supernatural strength and favor with God. We've seen how timing is everything and that for faith to grow time needs to tick off. We have learned to suffer with purpose because we desperately need purpose to survive. We've been set free by forgiveness, overcoming the bondage of bitterness. We've seen how God uses our chronic trial to develop deep relationships.

As we continued, we learned to overcome our fears through magnifying God rather than our circumstances. We hiked through hope when there seemed to be no hope. We saw the importance of getting things right by living in God's Word. Finally, we asked that the true worshippers arise and take your stand in worshipping the only worthy One.

My prayer is that you have obtained practical wisdom for your journey, or for the journey of one you know and care about. I pray that through the pain of suffering long term, with all of its facets and dynamics, you would be able to both survive and thrive inwardly in your relationship with God. I pray not only that you would hear *about* God, or know *of* Him, or merely be encouraged by someone else's experiences, but to actually experience God yourself. To be able to sing in your prison as Paul and Silas did in their dark hour.

So, maybe this is the most important chapter, because we all have *defining moments*—moments that give us opportunity to experience and glorify God in a unique way *because of* our suffering.

When we look at Job's amazing story, something very profound comes to our notice. After Job experienced incredible human loss and pain through the death of his children and servants; the loss of his wealth and livelihood; the loss of his health through relentless pain; the loss of his friends who turned on him; and after the spiritual battles of reconciling his suffering with what he'd heard about God; yes, after a whole book about human suffering, we find a very surprising ending. Yet, in this divine twist, we find the true unexpected answer we were looking for all the time—we just didn't know how to ask for it.

Oddly, God didn't directly answer any of Job's questions or the issues brought up by his friends. Yet, by revealing Himself to Job, God answered all of them. In Job, chapter 38, God plied *Job* with questions that Job wasn't expecting. The purpose of these questions was to shift Job's gaze and attention away from his own miserable suffering to the glorious God of the universe. God's penetrating questions not only answered all of Job's questions about suffering, but ours as well. By posing questions to Job that only God could answer, God moved Job from a position of miserable *victim* to triumphant *victor* as Job placed his footing fully on the solid rock of God's character.

What I'm saying is that when a man or woman with all their trials and suffering comes face to face with God Himself, that is enough. God is the answer to all our questions. When I see God and am rightly related to Him, that is really all I need to know. The massive, solid rock of His being and character is enough—yes, more than enough! Friends, when by faith we recognize God's sufficiency for us, we have all we need. Do we believe God is enough? Yes, one day soon when we stand before God we will know that. Just one glimpse of Him in all His glory will topple any other imposing question. When I see Him I will say, "Now I know." Every question will be answered clearly, even if no words are explained. Why? Because, God is my explanation. (See 2 Corinthians 12:7-10.)

Standing in God's presence and being confronted with His all-sufficiency was Job's defining moment. Job's realization of God's sufficiency and his humble response and trust in God newly defined his life. I know we are not Job. But you are who God created you to be. And your unique calling of suffering is just as important to God for His glory, which is worth it all. Again, none of us are looking for the 'pat' answers. We look for the bottom line, the ultimate answer—God Himself. He is the Answer. If He has allowed this pain in your life—define your moment—trust in Him and Him alone. Tell Him, "Lord, I accept this from Your hand. Help me to suffer well for Your honor. Be my Answer. You are enough." In God Himself is our sufficiency and the answers to all other questions.

In chapters 38 to 42 of Job, God helped Job to see that there is far more than meets the eye. It's as if God said, "Job, I am God and you are not. There are some things I know and can do that you don't know and can't do—trust me on this."

Your heart will beat approximately two-and-a-half billion times pumping sixty million gallons of blood—without resting—during your lifetime. You will take around 630 million breaths through your throat and into your lungs. When infection enters your body, white blood cells will gather and lay down their lives for you (just as Jesus did). "Job, the evidence is overwhelming—I see, I care and I defend." Contemplate for a moment the complexity of the human eye. "The human eye can distinguish millions of shades of color. On a clear dark night we can see a small candle flame from thirty miles away."[38] The cells and nerves and thoughts interacting through tens of millions of cells at one time are impossible to simulate on any computer. Look at the complexity of the ear. What could be said of the human brain? Who designed and put into place our soul, or our spirit? Even our fingers can detect a difference of .0004 inches thick. How about the functions of our emotions?

There are billions of atoms in our bodies. "To count the atoms in a drop of water would require every human on earth counting one atom, per second, for twenty thousand years."

What about the sub-atomic particles? What do we understand of anti-matter? Or consider the string theory where these rubber band like strings vibrate rhythmically. "A super-string loop is a hundred million billion times smaller than the nucleus of an atom."[39]

Take your eye off the microscope and look through the telescope. Think about it—God knows where every sub-atomic particle in the universe is located and how they all interact. A galaxy has billions of stars. There are thought to be billions of galaxies. God has named every star. How big is the universe? How many light years across? Do we fully understand time, space or light? How about gravity?

My mother taught me many things. Perhaps the most important was her view of how big God is. Not just in transcendent vastness, but also in detailed genius. "But do not overlook this one fact, beloved, that with the Lord, one day is as a thousand years, and a thousand years as one day." (2 Peter 3:8) I take that to mean, among other details, that to God, one day could be microscopically detailed as if a thousand years of circumstances. As well, a thousand years could telescopically be seen to God as if happening in one day. Either way, God is big—much bigger than we ever could imagine.

Like Job, our lifetimes are sandwiched as a thin line in a vast history. But God transcends time. Our minds are limited as is our understanding. We are unable to know or integrate *all* information. God's understanding is limitless. My strength is small. God hung the universe in place by speaking it into existence. My sense of justice and fairness, like that of Job's friends, is completely skewed by misunderstanding, lack of information and bias. Whereas, God is completely just and fair.

God asks, "Who then is he who can stand before Me?" (Job 41:10) God is so holy, so vast, who of us can stand before God without the mediating help of Jesus? "Who has first given to Me, that I should repay him? Whatever is under the whole heaven is Mine." (Job 41:11) Job can only respond:

> I know that You can do all things, and that no purpose of Yours can be thwarted. "Who is this that hides counsel without knowledge?" Therefore I have uttered what I did not understand, things too wonderful for me, which I did not know. "Hear, and I will speak; I will question you, and you make it known to me." I had heard of You by the hearing of the ear, but now my eye sees You; therefore, I despise myself and repent in dust and ashes." (Job 42:2-6)

I must confess, as I have been brought face to face with God in my trial, I've needed to repent, humble myself and acknowledge my great God.

When we say that God is enough, we don't mean that God is barely adequate or just satisfactory. What we do mean is that His sufficiency is plentiful, abundant, bountiful, complete and ample. Remember God's supply is not limited to our needs. By virtue of who He is, He is infinitely more than I need. I can only drink so much, but He is more vast than the ocean. "The Lord is my Shepherd; I have everything I need." (Psalm 23:1 NLT)

The concept of contentment has fallen on hard times in the confusion and so called "progress" of our culture. Yet, contentment is a very powerful grace. Genuine contentment says, "I have enough because I have God." (1 Timothy 6:6-8 NLT) Someone has said, "Enough is as good as a feast." And so it is with God.

When we allow contentment and gratefulness a place in our hearts we can enjoy the feast of "enough" all day. When enough is from the hand of a sovereign God we experience a satisfying fullness. When the satisfaction of contentment comes from God, He is our "enough." Feast your soul on God today. You can't eat tomorrow's meals today. Enjoy the feast of God's presence today. How is your appetite? "Taste and see that the Lord is good." (Psalm 34:8) We enjoy a good meal. Do we enjoy a good God? Food can satisfy our stomach; only God can satisfy our souls. His presence is a feast. "You will show me the way of life, granting me the joy of your presence and the pleasures of living with you forever." (Psalm 16:11 NLT)

When we sit down to eat a big meal we loosen our belt to enjoy more food. When the iron collar of pain and suffering is around our soul, we think we can't loosen it, and so it is. But we forget that the soul is not limited to the physical dimension. The soul has another dimension. It can expand even in those hard trials because God is spirit, and He can fill you. We "loosen" our soul to receive more of Him by our faith and trust.

Psalm 23 tells us that God sets the feast in front of us even in the midst of the battle. He restores our soul. We are reminded that "'enough" is God giving us richly from Himself all we need for our enjoyment. (1 Timothy 6:17 NLT) Contentment works when God is our *content*. Are you content in God? Is God enough? Are you feasting on God Himself? Your life depends on it.

We must remember that God has allowed us to see Him in the very face of Jesus. "For God, who said, 'Let light shine out of darkness,' has shone in our hearts to give the light of the knowledge of the glory of God in the face of Jesus Christ. The spot light is on Jesus." (2 Corinthians 4:6) The Creator is also our

Redeemer and His name is Jesus. "Blessed be the God and Father of our Lord Jesus Christ, who has blessed us *in Christ* with *every spiritual blessing* in the heavenly places." (Ephesians 1:3) Friend, if you are a follower of Jesus Christ your glass is neither half full nor half empty—it is full and overflowing.

So, "What shall we say to these things? If God is for us, who can be against us? He who did not spare His own Son, but gave Him up for us all, how will He not also with Him graciously give us all things?" (Romans 8:31-32) Please read and re-read that one! The Godhead knows and sympathizes in our pain. The Father suffered in the offering of His Son and the Son suffered by allowing His soul to enter the iron of our sin. Think of the sacrifice and suffering His soul experienced as the sinless One took our sins upon Himself. Nails, iron nails, pierced His body. An iron sword pierced His side. The Holy Spirit helps us to understand these things by taking up residence as a spring of living water. The Godhead has entered our souls.

Is it well with your soul? When Oprah, who is simply a spokeswoman for our culture, says that there are ways other than Jesus to get to God, don't you think that is an infinite slap in the face to God? She is declaring, in essence, that Jesus is not enough. Piled on top of all our other sins, the ultimate sin would be rejecting Jesus. But friend, if God didn't spare His Son but gave Him up for us, can we recognize that all our other needs will be freely supplied by Him as well? Again, if and when we ever doubt, one thing we can be assured of is that Jesus loves us and cares for us.

Paul reminds us, "Not that we are sufficient in ourselves to claim...anything as coming from us, but our sufficiency is from God." (2 Corinthians 3:5) So dear friend, see and savor God. He is abundantly able; let Him be your all. Let His character and presence stand as your answer. We can trust Him for the unknowns because He already gave us His most precious gift, His own Son, Jesus. Look long and well into the face of Jesus.

> "Jesus, I am resting, resting
>   In the Joy of what Thou art;
> I am finding out the greatness
>   Of Thy loving heart.
> Thou hast bid me gaze upon Thee,
>   And Thy beauty fills my soul,
> For by Thy transforming power
>   Thou hast made me whole."[40]

Remember that the greatest thing you can do for your own well-being is to love the Lord your God. God writes the last chapter, we don't. Let us rest in His sufficiency. Let us finally be satisfied with Him. Let Him be our delight and joy. That will be your defining moment.

In the dark night of the soul, worship God with belief and obedience and thanksgiving and praise. There is great wisdom in suffering for it propels us to God.

"The grace of the Lord Jesus Christ and the love of God and the fellowship of the Holy Spirit be with you all." (2 Corinthians 13:14)

Chapter 19.
The Sacrament of Life Change

As Christ-followers, when all is well and we are healthy and not too distracted by pain and suffering, we tend to think we need to work "for" God. By nature, we tend to rely on our abilities, strength and know-how. When all is not well, the rug is pulled out from under us, and the chronic pain sets in, we lose strength and stamina and we tend to move from a work-for-God mindset to a more rest-in-God position. "I don't have the strength; so I'll just 'let' God work."

The funny thing is that both of the above perspectives are biblical. Christian writers, teachers and theologians have struggled with this balance since Christ returned to heaven. "What is God's part and what is my part?" We *trust and obey*. We *rest and work*. We let God be God, yet we are truly responsible and held accountable for our part. Maybe in certain situations God allows us to move more one way and then the other. Maybe in His great love, as He works to bring about life changes in us, He allows us at times to be more aware of His work and our rest in that. Then at other times, He makes us more aware of the work of our response to Him. As I've observed life, I see this pattern often. Maybe in our relationships we need to be more understanding and kind with one another as we all bounce off of center toward one extreme or the other.

A couple of years ago, I saw this dual perspective in Genesis, "When Abram was 99 years old, the Lord appeared to him, saying, 'I am God Almighty. Live in My presence and be devout.'" (Genesis 17:1 HCSB) This balance of life change seems to surface as far back as Genesis. What do we learn here? One is never too old to experience life-change. Abram was 99. Because of our condition, the Lord is always the sovereign initiator. None of us, including Abram, could know God without His revelation to us. God is at work long before we know or respond.

Next, we see in this passage that God is ALMIGHTY. He is the great I AM, the eternally existing One, totally sufficient in Himself. He doesn't need anything, including us. That may bother some, but when we realize two things, it's actually reassuring. First, God is perfect and complete in Himself. That is a very good thing for us. God has no needs. We need a God like that. Second, He may not need us, but He passionately *wants* us anyway. We see the extent of that in the offering and sacrifice of His only Son to save us from our sins.

So, getting back to Genesis 17:1, God told our faith-father Abram, "Live in My presence." What an amazing invitation! God seeks a personal, intimate love relationship with us, as the rest of Scripture explains as well. Stop and think about the incredible blessing and favor God bestows on us to invite us to live in His presence. Jesus said He came to give us abundant life— a full, overflowing, purposeful, meaningful existence. It starts here on planet earth by a faith relationship and continues forever. Because God is eternal, our life enters His eternal life. Are you consciously aware of God's presence in your life?

But this brings up the issue we're discussing. Can anyone live in God's presence, or to put it another way, can anyone have the presence of God activated by His Son and animated by His Spirit living in us, and not be changed? Praise the Lord! Jesus mediates the relationship. He reconciles us to God. Then, He very reasonably asks us to "be devout," or give Him our whole-hearted devotion. Our part is to live in His presence as a disciplined follower of Him. To be loyally devoted to God becomes a reality as we live out the consequences of living in God's presence and according to His claims and promises. To be devout is a life mingled with fear and love, of reverence and joy, of work and rest. It is the practical response to God's practical initiation.

When we believe, we become disciples of Christ, devoted and disciplined followers of Jesus. My brother Rob, in one of his books, calls this "dependent-diligence."[41] It is the living out, of His presence living in. There is both a rest in or *dependence* on God, and simultaneously a life of *diligent* devotion to Him. Would such living not necessitate life-change in us? If God is perfect, holy and unchanging, of rock solid character, would it not seem appropriate and necessary that I should be changed—transformed by Him as I dwell in His presence? God's presence with me would also motivate me to be devoted, committed, loyal, ardent, concerned, consecrated, fervent, faithful and determined in my relationship with Him. Is it not reasonable to dedicate our spirit, soul and body to Him by faith both depending on Him and being devoted to Him?

Let's look at it from another angle. As a chronic sufferer, you may not only feel like a dependent receiver all the time, but your life may actually bear it out. In one sense, as followers of Jesus, we live all of our daily lives by simply receiving. We read, "Indeed, we have all received grace after grace from His fullness." (John 1:16 HCSB) God gives us grace to get up in the morning. As we awake, God gives us grace to think about and enjoy Him. He then graces us for each task and concern of the day and so on. Maybe that's one reason that the Christian life is so offensive to many. We are needy receivers. We are helpless without Him. We need Him for our next breath. So, when we suffer, we are simply reminded to an even greater extent that without Him we can do nothing. Yet, through Christ we can do all things with His strength working through us.

As the suffering continues and doesn't let up, we've seen how it can affect many other areas of our lives, like finances. We may become quite needy financially because of the nature of the trial. We are deeply humbled and find ourselves needing help. God begins to provide favor and blessing layer upon layer. The prayer for removal of the main pain doesn't seem answered, but many "smaller" prayers are answered on an hourly and daily basis. As we learn to become humble receivers from the hand of God, we begin to change from the inside out. Our pride and anger get exposed and we soften and sense God's presence. As God uses others to provide kindness, money, prayers, hospitality, service or meals we feel awkward at first. We've been so *independent*—now we are so *dependent*—we change because of our dependence on God and others.

In the past we said we love God. Now we begin to show it by obedience to His Word and His promptings. Inner change flowing from His abiding presence begins to transform our character. The hard edges become smoother. We realize the truth that we are all recipients of God's amazing grace on a daily basis and the chronic sufferer may experience this realization to a greater degree.

Jesus said, "It's more blessed to give than to receive." (Acts 20:35) How do we reconcile that statement with our needy, ever-receiving lives? If you look at the context of those words by Jesus, Paul is talking about supporting the weak, and the blessing and happiness that can bring. We find a great practical commentary on this subject in Luke 12:16-31.

Yet, Paul reminds us of the fact we are all God-graced recipients, "What makes you better than anyone else? What do you have that God hasn't given you? And if all you have is from God, why boast as though you have accomplished something on your own?" (1 Corinthians 4:7 NLT) Every good and perfect gift comes from God. God gives health, wealth, people, skills, talents and wisdom, etc. So why does Paul remind us of Jesus' words that one is happier when giving than receiving? Maybe it is because receiving is simply necessary and humbling. Yet, receiving a kind word, a financial gift in time of need, a meal when you return from the hospital, finding that someone mowed your lawn and so on, is also a great blessing. We are not to stop there, Jesus says. The fuller blessing comes as we graciously receive and then use that as a platform to bless others. It is better to give than receive, because giving is focused on blessing others, rather than self. But there is also great grace in receiving, when it is performed for the benefit of others.

Have you ever visited a friend in the hospital with the intention of cheering them up only to leave having received a blessing yourself? I believe we, as chronic suffering recipients, greatly underestimate the blessings we can give to others in gifts of: a cheerful smile in our pain; a thankful and grateful spirit; a word of encouragement; a persevering faith and hope example, etc. You see the gift goes on. Your blessing of receiving from others and God is passed on to others in different forms of encouragement. Your gift of attitude toward God and others can be a blessing far beyond any monetary receiving. The sacrifice of your service to others, even in a joyful smile, can bring great blessing. Instead of merely being *containers* of blessing, we can be *conduits* of blessing. Share the loveJ It can change lives. (See 2 Corinthians 9:12.)

Some writers of the past have called all this the sacrament of living. A sacrament is an external expression of an inward grace. Remembering the Lord's Supper in the cup and bread is an outward expression of an inward grace transformation. The Lord's Supper reminds us of not only His sacrifice of body and blood, but how His sacrifice has made a difference in our lives. The sacrament of baptism expresses to God and others how Jesus' death, burial and resurrection have impacted and changed our lives.

In the same way, our humble trust in Christ and our diligent obedience to Him are sacramental expressions of all that God has given us in Christ. "So whether you eat or drink, or whatever you do, do all to the glory of God." (1 Corinthians 10:31) This is priestly living—coming to daily life with the same reverence and passion as we would for communion or baptism.

If you have suffered deeply, you know that suffering reduces life to mundane living activities. We shift to survival mode—the bare essentials. Yet, because of the transforming presence of Jesus in our life, who is our very life, suffering can also raise life to kingdom living activities. Simple, seemingly insignificant activities can become sacraments of glorious life change. We must both allow this process and pursue it. God's presence must flow in our blood. By His grace we can experience courageous devotion.

Life change is an attitude of receiving grace lived out in devoted determination. I choose to honor God by living in His presence. God has chosen to bless me with life in His presence. This life-change often comes with the grace of chronic pain.

This life transformation can be unnerving, uneasy, and uncomfortable. The Bible calls it a death-resurrection process. The seed falls into the ground alone, buried and dead, and yet by life from God grows into a fruitful plant. This is the process of God; it is absolutely necessary because of our condition. God is preparing us for an eternity of life in His presence. Let us be aggressive in our faith. Let us be courageous in our waiting. Let us be cooperative with our God. Let us be thankful, grateful, cheerful and receptive. Let us be steadfast and faithful. Let us finish the fight well. Let us lean hard against the reliable character of God in times of uncertainty. John reminds us, "Dear children, keep away from anything that might take God's place in your hearts." (1 John 5:21 NLT)

Remember Jesus' words, "Are you tired? Worn out? Burned out on religion? Come to Me. Get away with Me and you'll recover your life. I'll show you how to take a real rest. Walk with Me and work with Me—watch how I do it. Learn the unforced rhythms of grace. I won't lay anything heavy or ill-fitting on you. Keep company with Me and you'll learn to live freely and lightly." (Matthew 11:28-30 MSG)

All eyes and hearts should be on Jesus. Accept His invitation. Recover your life—let Him restore your soul. Rest in His finished work. Walk, work and watch with Jesus. Hear His heartbeat—lean in close—live in His presence—be free and lighten your load. Go with Him.

The tale is told of a man who was bearing the burden of a heavy back pack as he trudged along a dusty road. When a man in a wagon came by and offered the weary man a ride, he gladly accepted the offer and climbed on the wagon. Yet, when the driver urged him to take the pack off his back and lay it in the cart, the weary traveler responded, "Oh no. You've been so gracious to give me a ride, I couldn't possibly ask you to carry my pack too."

Many of us live like that burdened man, unable to receive what God has already given us. "He who did not spare His own Son but gave Him up for us all, how will He not also, with Him, graciously give us all things?" (Romans 8:32) "Cast all your cares upon Him because He cares for you." (1 Peter 5:7) "Therefore, let those who suffer according to God's will, entrust their souls to a faithful Creator while doing good." (1 Peter 4:19) "And after you have suffered a little while, the God of all grace, who has called you to His eternal glory in Christ, *will Himself* restore, confirm, strengthen, and establish you. To Him be the dominion forever and ever. Amen." (1 Peter 5:10) We are not victims. We are victors in Christ. The Lord bless you on your journey. The glory of God is worth it all!

Chapter 20.
The Last Chapter

The last chapter may be the end of this book but it is definitely not the end of the story. God Himself writes the last chapter. Joseph saw this as he talked with his brothers who had abandoned him and sold him into slavery. "As far as I am concerned, God turned into good what you meant for evil. He brought me to *the high position* I have today, so I could save the lives of many people." (Genesis 50:20 NLT)

The New Testament sheds further light on Joseph's story, "These sons of Jacob were very jealous of their brother Joseph, and they sold him to be a slave in Egypt. But God was with him and *delivered him from his anguish*." (Acts 7:9-10 NLT)

Yes, the story ended quite well for Joseph. He was reconciled with his family; he saved at least two nations from starvation; and God delivered him from his soul anguish.

We say, "That's great for him, but things haven't worked out so well for me." The pain has not let up for years; the disease looks terminal. The torture and persecution continues. The confinement and loneliness persists. My story isn't ending so well.

Remember, however, even though some things turned around for Joseph, not everything did. Other than once, to bury his father in the Promised Land, Joseph could not leave Egypt. He died a slave, yes, an exalted slave, but still a slave to

Pharaoh. He could not go back and live in the Promised Land of God's blessing. At the end of Genesis, we see how important the Promised Land was to Joseph, "He made an oath with the sons of Israel to swear that: 'When God comes to lead us back to Canaan, you must take my body back with you.' So, Joseph died at the age of 110. They embalmed him and his body was placed in a coffin in Egypt." (Genesis 50:25-26 NLT) Some 400 years later when Moses led the Israelites out of Egypt, they took Joseph's bones with them and buried them in the Promised Land in keeping with Joseph's request.

God is sovereign—we are not. The story is not about *us*. It is about *God*, who He is, what He says, what He does. It is a redemptive story that on every page of history sees the finger prints of God, for the sole purpose of bringing Him great glory. It's not about us—it's about His glory. Your suffering is not about you, but about God's glory.

The Author of life has chosen to write us into the script and we each have a part, a very important part. Do you know your lines? Lines like, "I trust You, Lord." "Thank You, Lord." "I need You, Lord." "Lord, glorify Yourself through my trial." "I worship You." "I don't understand my circumstances, I don't even like them, but I trust You." "Glory to God in the highest." Or maybe your script just calls for one word—"Help!" You cry out to God in ultimate dependence—"Help!" Yet, by that cry of a soul in deep anguish, you tap in to the glory of the Most High God.

Again, though Joseph lived and died a slave in Egypt, God did deliver his soul from the anguish of the trial. The collar of suffering may remain on your neck, but the Lover of your soul can deliver you in it, from the meaningless anguish. And, yes, He is able, as the God of the impossible, to replace that soul-anguish with His own joy. Joseph's soul entered the iron, "Until the time came to fulfill His word, the Lord tested Joseph's character." (Psalm 105:19 NLT) God can and may release you from your trial at any time, or He may choose to release you in death. Either way, in life or in death, to God be the glory.

"With joy you will drink deeply from the fountain of salvation." (Isaiah 12:3) When you drink deeply and feast on God Himself that is enough. The Savior who was full of joy because of His perfect union with the Father was also a "man of sorrows and acquainted with grief." (Isaiah 53:3)

Dear friend, you are not alone. Many fellow sufferers are on the trail ahead and behind you. Be encouraged in the Lord. The Savior has gone ahead of us, but He has come back to help carry us. God is with you. Remember, He is the "Author and Finisher of our faith." (Hebrews 12:2) He is the A to Z, the first and last and everything in between.

The story ends well for all Jesus' followers. Take courage and persevere. As you continue your journey, I leave with you a few verses from Psalm 73:

> Then I realized how bitter I had become, how pained I had been by all I had seen. I was so foolish and ignorant—I must have seemed like a senseless animal to you. Yet, I still belong to you; You are holding my right hand. You will keep on guiding me with your counsel, leading me to a *glorious destiny*. Whom have I in heaven but *You*? I desire *You* more than anything on earth. My health may fail, and my spirit may grow weak, but God remains the strength of my heart; He is mine forever.— But those who desert Him, will perish, for you destroy those who abandon You. But as for me, how good it is to be near God! I have made the sovereign Lord my shelter,

and I will tell everyone about the wonderful things You do. (Psalm 73:21-28 NLT)

As we close this book, I am reminded of another little known detail of Joseph's story. After thirteen years of imprisonment, he interpreted Pharaoh's dream and was elevated overnight to second in command in Egypt. Sometime during the first seven years of plenty before the great seven years of famine, Joseph was given a wife, Asenath, the daughter of Potiphera, priest of Heliopolis. From that marriage were born two sons whose names are significant and provide insight.

The first was Manasseh meaning, "God has made me forget all my troubles and the family of my father." (Genesis 41:51 NLT) I don't think he meant that he never thought about his family back in the Promised Land. It seems that God graced Joseph with a certain divine amnesia to the pain of the past. I have seen God do that with chronic sufferers, that is, give them a fresh mental start that somehow diminishes the pain of the past.

The second son was named Ephraim, meaning, "God has made me fruitful in this land of my suffering." (Genesis 41:52 NLT) Joseph remained in the land of suffering, yet God made him fruitful in the midst of it.

I believe God can make each of us fruitful in our place of suffering. He can grace us with fresh attitudes of love, joy, peace, patience, kindness, goodness, faithfulness, gentleness and self-control. This is the fruit of the abiding Holy Spirit in us, animating the righteous life of Jesus Christ *through us*.

Dear friend, the last chapter is a glorious one! Lean hard against the powerful character of God in a surrendered restful position. It's not how big our faith is, but how big our God is in whom we rest our small faith.

And remember: God is enough, simply because He is God! Do you believe this?

Author Bio

Mark Fischer currently lives in Spokane, Washington with his wife, Denese. Mark is a graduate of Moody Bible Institute, Spokane, WA. Mark spent 15 years in the medical field as an orthotist and 15 years as a pastor, mostly serving with Village Missions in Washington, Idaho and Montana. They currently attend Northview Bible Church in Spokane, WA.

Mark and Denese have four grown children and ten grandchildren. Mark still finds God to be enough as he continues in his trial of suffering.

———————————————————————

To order more copies of this book, please log onto <u>www.Amazon.com</u> and other online retailers. If you have found encouragement and hope in reading this book, please consider telling others about this book on Facebook or other social networks.

Endnotes

1   Charles Spurgeon, *The Treasury of David*. Vol. 2, p. 351.

2   See Genesis 37-50.

3   Genesis 37:2, 3, 5-11

4   Genesis 37:2

5   Genesis 37:20

6   Genesis 41:46

7   1 Thessalonians 3:3

8   John of Avila, *NIV Worship Bible*, p. 1499.

9   Anne Graham-Lotz, "Why."

10   Job 30:16-31; 2:10

11   Charles Swindoll, *The Mystery of God's Will*, p. 208.

12   J.B. Phillips, *New International Worship Bible*, p. 158.

13   Max Lucado, www.goodreads.com/author/quotes/2737. Max Lucado.

14   Dietrich Bonhoeffer as quoted by Adele A. Cahoun, *Spiritual Disciplines Handbook*, (Donners Grove, IL: IVP Books, 2005) p. 111.

15   *The Works of Josephus* translated by William Whiston, (Peabody, MA: Hendrickson Publishers, 1987), p.286.

16   NIV Worship Bible, p. 1478.

17   NIV Worship Bible, p. 1039.

18   Tony Evans, *Who is this King of Glory?* (Chicago: Moody Press, 1999) p. 165.

19   Pamela Reeve, *Faith Is* (Three Sisters, OR: Multnomah Press, 1994).

20   Warren Wiersbe, *Why Us?*, (Old Tappan, NJ: Fleming H. Revell Co., 1985), p. 11.

21   Pamela Reeve, *Faith Is*, (Three Sisters, OR: Multnomah Press, 1994).

22   Warren Wiersbe, *Why Us?*, (Old Tappan, NJ: Fleming H. Revell Co., 1985), p. 12.

23   A.W.Tozer, *The Knowledge of the Holy*, (Lincoln, NE: Back to the Bible Broadcast, 1961), p. 113.

24   Acts 4:12; John 14:6; Romans 10:3.

25   Warren Wiersbe, *Old Testament Prophet Commentary*, (Colorado Springs: Victor, 2002), p. 223.

26   Charles Spurgeon (source unknown).

27   Denese Fischer, *In Your Presence*—a poem.

28   Eugene Petersen, *Run with the Horses*, (InterVarsity Press: Downers Grove, IL, 2009), p. 98.

29   Warren Wiersbe, *Why Us?* (Old Tappan, NJ: Fleming H. Revell Co., 1985), p.51.

30   Source unknown.

31   Warren Wiersbe, *Why Us?*, (Old Tappan, NJ: Fleming H. Revell Co., 1985), p. 41 & 51.

32   I'd like to give credit to Institute in Basic Youth Conflicts (IBYC) for this quote and some of the ideas presented here.

33   John McArthur, *The Freedom and Power of Forgiveness*, (Crossway Books: Wheaton, IL, 1998), p. 211.

34   John McArthur.

35   *The Doxology.*

36   A.W. Tozer, *Knowledge of the Holy*, (New York: HarperCollins, 1961), p. 7.

37   *The Doxology.*

38   Richard Swenson, M.D., *More than Meets the Eye*, (Colorado Springs, NAVPRESS, 2000).

39   Richard Swenson, M.D.

40   Jean Sophia Pigotti, *Jesus, I am Resting, Resting,* 1876.

41   Rob Fischer, *Enthralled with God*, (Bloomington, IN: WestBow Press, 2010).

Made in the USA
Charleston, SC
28 July 2012